Rainier Sojourn

Around Rainier on The Wonderland Trail

By

DANIEL A. SAVIERS

*This book is dedicated to my father,
who taught me about hard work and
commitment to family and community,
encouraged my whims of exploration, and
gave me freedom to grow.*

Rainier Sojourn

Introduction

Two hundred and fifty miles out to sea from Washington and Oregon, hidden from view by the deep turquoise waters of the Pacific Ocean, a geologic event of the grandest scale is transpiring, shaping the continental stage where we act out our lives. The seafloor is splitting apart and magma pours forth from the rift, some of it flowing west to attach to the Pacific tectonic plate, and the remainder surging eastward to enlarge the Juan de Fuca plate. The irreversible impetus drives the latter mass, at the rate of an inch a year, into a headlong collision with the westward-tending North American plate.

The titanic struggle between the fifty-mile thick plates is initiated sixty miles off the shores of the Northwestern United States. At the impact site, named the Cascadia subduction zone, the lighter continental crust rides over the more dense oceanic plate, with the latter veering downward at a sixty-five-degree angle toward its inevitable destiny of being recycled back into the molten deep mantle—180 miles below the surface. It submerges hesitantly (taking four million years to travel from the subduction zone to a position underneath the Cascade Mountains), with the resistant lurches resonating as earthquakes. Ocean floor sediment, accumulated through the eons, is scraped off the subducting plate and mingles with water and substance of the upper mantle, which is wedged between the competing structures; the aggregate is then brought to a boil by the profound heat of friction. The resulting magma, which is relatively lighter, rises eighty miles through cracks in the subterranean realm, eventually to explode through the surface, birthing a volcanic mountain range, the Cascades—a land of delight, and fear.

The Cascade Range extends from Mount Lassen in Northern California, through Oregon and Washington, to Mount Garibaldi in Southern British Columbia. Along the way are well-known natural wonders, which are sources of inspiration and physical challenge: Mount Shasta, Crater Lake, the Three Sisters, Mount Hood, Mount St. Helens, Mount Rainier, and the North Cascades. The string includes many precipitous, rugged peaks that challenge the skill of mountain climbers, while between the cloud-piercing luminaries are an extensive carpet of pumice deserts, mysterious forests, and glorious meadows that test the prowess of orienteers.

Mount Rainier is perhaps the most formidable opponent, whether scaling its airy summit or clamoring up and down the steep valleys along its flanks. Upon its shoulders are a variety of environments, compacted into such a small land area that an astounding landscape is created. As John Muir described in *Our National Parks*, "Of all the fire-mountains...Mount Rainier is the noblest in form.... Its massive white dome rises out of its forests, like a world by itself.... The forests reach to a height of a little over six thousand feet, and above the forests there is a zone of the loveliest flowers, fifty miles in circuit and nearly two miles wide, so closely planted and luxuriant that it seems as if Nature, glad to make an open space between woods so dense and ice so deep, were economizing the precious ground, and trying to see how many of her darlings she can get together in one mountain wreath...." Rainier is an icon of the Northwest, as recognized as the Seattle Space Needle or the Columbia River, wound into geologic and human history, and hence inspiring a plethora of tales of existence by all who have been privileged to live in the shadow of its grandeur. Soaring into the stratosphere, it authors its own climate and nourishes an astonishing diversity of plant and animal life—that my best friend and I attempted to decipher with the aid of several guidebooks.

Our pilot was the Wonderland Trail, which ascends and descends through the varied ecosystems, reverently winding its way around the base of the mighty volcano. When my best friend, Patrick, and I departed for Mount Rainier, in late August 1997, our ambitions were not merely to view the lavish floral displays and risk encountering violent lava flows, but, more accurately, to fulfill personal accomplishments. This trek would be Patrick's first extended backpacking trip (and I felt like a proud mentor ready to watch my pupil pass a major examination), and the completion of the vaunted loop would be another check off my list of things to accomplish during this lifetime. So we arrived at Mount Rainier National Park with the demeanor of conquerors, and this was a worthy antagonist. Our two-week assault would culminate months of experimentation, planning, and wonder, but during the extensive preparation I failed to consider the real reason I return to the wilderness, again and again—to reconnect to the living universe.

A sojourn around Mount Rainier is a demanding physical catechism, but the many splendors observed and cataloged along the passage refresh the spirit. Prior to our departure, we investigated, in some detail, the anticipated terrain about Rainier and the Wonderland Trail, including access routes and accommodations; however, in retrospect, this was more of a forensic analysis. In order to agree on an itinerary, altitude gains and losses were plotted, the favorable attributes of each potential campsite were envisaged, and the logistics of hiking various distances with heavy packs on our backs were pondered. Menus were devised, food and drink procured; equipment was prepared, bought, mended, and reviewed for its benefit versus its weight, before being stowed within our backpacks. We daydreamed about the beauty of the diverse locales, as illuminated in the guidebooks; and indeed, once we were on the trail, the wildflowers were a kaleidoscope of color and fragrance, the chickadees sang sweet melodies, the milky-white rivers were adrenaline-pumping and spectacular, and the luminous dome of Rainier was our constant companion. However, what the guidebooks cannot adequately describe is the effect that the odyssey will have on your soul. The profound joy, contemplation, and serenity experienced with every footfall.

The revelation that was perhaps most striking, and unanticipated, to me was to be apprehended in the unmistakable handiwork of unresting evolution, perpetually transforming the world. Usually when I contemplate a grand mountain, notions of strength, stability, and permanence come to mind, but not at Rainier. Each valley, meadow, glacier, and stream was in transition; even the volcano exuded change. Old-growth forest thrived in the wet, temperate, western canyons, with fallen giants being consumed by the microbial inhabitants, and a new generation of trees springing from the humus. Every river traversed had a story to disclose about its turmoil and peace: trees buried in its banks, battered boulders transiently at rest in its wide gravely bed, and chill silty water cascading down from a lofty glacier. The ice fields themselves had evidence of prior assaults and subsequent withdrawals, leaving behind sweeping pumice-strewn moraines. Vast meadows of sedges and wildflowers were being infiltrated by fir and hemlock, transitioning back into forest. Grand amphitheaters, such as Sunrise, are spectacular arenas to visit, and live, but simultaneously hint of the explosive history of this peak. Rainier is alive! We were fortunate enough to witness a few breaths of the mountain: avalanches, rockslides, winds whipping up the precipitous slopes that sculpt gnarled krummholz, and glaciers rumbling through the night as they grind stone into powder that washes to the sea. Fires have scorched countless acres of verdant forest, leaving in their wake a stand of silvery trunks and fashioning stunning meadows of bear grass and huckleberries. I did not feel loss there, only transition.

The historical transgressions of human interlopers, in their fervent efforts to make Tacoma (Mount Rainier) safe to humanity, were also readily apparent. The original inhabitants, Native Americans, prospered on the diverse bounty afforded, though their nonbelligerent way of life has been erased, and only their names remind us of their existence: Nisqually, Ohanepecoch, Yakama. In the last several centuries Russian, Spanish, British, and American pioneers not only explored this region, but plopped down a few forts nearby and industriously endeavored to make the wilderness "safe" for the eventual invasion of permanent European-heritage residents.

As a people long removed from acquaintance and dependence on the natural world, "settlers" energetically transformed the landscape into the image of "western" humanity, an enterprise caustic to the mountain, which continues to this day. They freely applied their names to the rivers, peaks, and glaciers that they "conquered." It seems that the strategy of this culture is to be the master of the world, eliminating wilderness where other species might challenge their preeminence. The western world cringes from the dark forest, the fanged creatures, the chilling frost, and the rumbling thunderstorm, and henceforth constructs artificial domains of concrete and steel to smother the ground, glass to keep out the winds, dams to tame the waters, and natural gas pipelines into homes to eliminate any dependence on fire—and thereby are convinced of its control of the environment. Our need for a perception of safety and self-determination has successfully protected us from most natural dangers on a day-to-day basis, but the lack of direct contact with the elements of Nature separates us from our primary source of spirituality, and we become despondent.

Sure, the asphalt highways provide for easy access to Rainier, but they seem like deep lacerations into the mountain's flesh, though even these can be scabbed over when abandoned, as we observed along the North Puyallup and Carbon Rivers. The tenements of society abide at Paradise, Longmire, and Sunrise; however, they have been swallowed up in the remote reaches of Indian Henry's Hunting Ground. The multitude of souls that we encountered, crawling along the shoulders of Rainier only skimming the surface of grandeur, still have the mien of subjugators; here to summit, snap a few pictures from the safety of their car, drift tentatively into a meadow to pick flowers, or race around the base. (We met many resolute hikers, intent on circling the volcano in record time, and comparing timetables with us in an erstwhile competition.) Only a few folks, families, and friends come together in the quiet of the backcountry to reacquaint themselves with each other, and the wilderness.

Those who have never been on an extended backpacking trip into the wilderness, may wonder, "What do you do out there?" The oversimplified answer is that I find myself. Interacting with human beings, wildlife, and the mountain helps me discern who I am; at penultimate, it is a reaffirmation of the bond between the living world and me. I come nearer the truth of life, my place in the ecosystem, and joyfully acknowledge just how codependent I am with the remainder of existence. I wonder why we fear our origins, instead of finding comfort in the bosom of the universe. Removed from the contrived restraints of the "civilized" world, the truth and magnificence of the cosmos is palpable.

Of course, Patrick and I are not the first acculturated persons to discover peace and purpose in Nature. Henry David Thoreau noted in 1864 in *The Maine Woods*, "...not only for strength, but for beauty, the poet must, from time to time, travel the logger's path and the Indian's trail, to drink at some new and more bracing fountain of the Muses, far in the recesses of the wilderness." Mankind has time and again turned to the natural world, though admittedly with some initial trepidation, for comfort and meaning, returning to the roots of humanity upon the plains and in the woods of prehistory. Perhaps it is only in abandoning the contrived habitat of humankind that we can rediscover the authentic purpose for our existence, whispered by the wind through the pine boughs and mumbled by the boulders bouncing along the bed of a glacial river. *Homo sapiens* are not the masters of the universe, but are enmeshed in its fabric. We did not evolve in isolation from the physical planet, but as an integral part of it, though not the keystone. Casting aside the baggage of civilization, abandoning the fossil fuel–powered automobiles at the trailhead, each stride into the primeval forest brings one in closer contact to that which makes us human—and long-buried primitive instincts resurface.

I hope that the reader will enjoy reading about our journey around the base of a living volcano, Mount Rainier. I have done my best to describe the physical struggles—sweat, fatigue, aches—and mental rewards, painted amid the forests and meadows. The human interactions were real and not fabricated; though perhaps not dramatic, they have prompted internal reflection and growth. From the description of rumbling glaciers, roaring waterways, crashing avalanches, and the aftermath of tremendous landslides, I intend to portray the sense of the mountain as alive—for that is how it felt to Patrick and me. Most of all, I have attempted to depict the inseparability of past, present, and future, with our lives, our atoms, and our souls in a perpetual quest for self-improvement and enlightenment, interlinked with all eternity. Henceforth, whenever we contemplate the effects of past human intervention at any location, we realize the impact of our present actions, and strive to live at peace with the universe into the future, and not solely try to conquer it.

Have a pleasant voyage.

In The Beginning

"The John Muir Trail, North Cascades Park, or Mount Rainier." That was my answer to Patrick's question about where I would like to go on a two-week backpacking trip.

"So what's so special about those places?" Patrick's eyes scrunch slightly and his forehead furrows, as he envisions the three localities. This is more than a theoretical question, as we both have already scheduled two weeks free from any commitments in early September of this year.

I also squint to sum up what I have heard or read about those wildlands. "Well, North Cascades is so remote that hardly anyone goes there, and it is wild enough that we might even bump into a grizzly bear or two." That possibility sends a shiver down my spine.

"Cool," Patrick reflexively responds, but I can tell that he is not thrilled about stumbling upon a great brown bear with nowhere to run or hide.

Therefore, I quickly change the subject. "And the John Muir Trail passes through Evolution Valley, which looks incredible in pictures. I definitely want to see it with my own eyes before I die," I conclude emphatically; that determination is indeed true.

"Where's that again?" Patrick appears more hopeful.

"High in the Sierra near Sequoia. Mostly above tree line."

His face relaxes, but then tightens up again. "That sounds pretty good, but haven't you already done something like that?"

Well he has me there. "Not exactly. I've done a few Sierra Club trips near there, but it's not the same." Truth is, I've glimpsed Evolution Valley from a distance, but that did not satisfy my craving; instead, it only increased my desire to set my feet upon the grass in its wondrous meadows. Besides, the entire John Muir Trail is over two hundred miles in length, and I don't want this trip to purely be an athletic event.

"Well, I'd rather go somewhere that will be new to both of us."

"That's cool. I've never been to either of the others," I assure him. No use arguing the point.

"Rainier sounds good, but I don't really want to climb." Patrick is a bit dejected in finding fault with all three possibilities.

I chuckle while responding. "Me neither, but the Wonderland Trail loops around it. I read an article about it in *Backpacker*." Highlighted with photographs of wildflower-filled meadows and suspension bridges, the essay propelled Rainier onto my short list of treks to complete before I die.

"And you've never been to Rainier?" Patrick peers at me earnestly.

"Never on the trail," I am quick to reply, but then dutifully confess, "I've driven through a small part of the park."

That disclosure doesn't dampen his exuberant grin. "That sounds like the best of the three." With a mutual nod, our quest for Rainier and the Wonderland Trail is launched; two glorious September weeks to circle the massive volcano.

Ohio Farm

The majority of people that I interact with, including my family, imagine why I backpack anyway. Camping without access to electric, , a flush toilet, or showers, even if it is beside their automobile, is primitive enough for them, so that, by comparison, a two-week backpacking trip around Mount Rainier is quite absurd. Of course, it is not something that you just wake up one day and decide to do. (With the exception of those few fearless and reckless types who just do it. I am not of that persuasion, so long-distance trekking into the backcountry has evolved throughout my lifetime.)

My love for the wilds was inaugurated during my childhood on an Ohio dairy farm. The vast fields, hardwood forests, and even abandoned strip mines provided an inexhaustible resource of outdoor exploration opportunities for an imaginative youngster, even if it wasn't true wilderness. The woods were easy to escape into, between milking cows, feeding chickens, and baling hay. There I could search for pheasant nests and marvel at the newborn chicks. Mighty largemouth bass and feisty bluegills thrived in the stripper cuts, just waiting to bite the worm at the end of my fishing line. Deer secreted in the woodlands and I tracked them stealthily. Each autumn the mallards and Canada geese would make a temporary appearance—stimulating daydreams about the far north from which they were flying, and the deep south to which they were heading. As frost nipped the inflamed maple leaves from their resident twigs, I trapped muskrat, beaver, and raccoon from Little Beaver Creek. (Though I am not as proud of that avocation now as I was then.) Best of all, the farmstead nurtured fantasies of surviving on the frontier and hollow trees served as hideouts, in case I got ambushed. I constructed secret forts and pretended to be self-sufficient—subsisting off the land by my own wits.

My mother blames my exploratory nature on my father's genetics, for the reason that the Saviers have roamed far and wide through the centuries. Immigrating to the American Colonies in the early 1700s, they had pushed west with the frontier, and by the 1850s several clans had reached the wildlands of California, although my more immediate ancestors remained on their farms in Ohio and western Pennsylvania.

The adventurous blood spirit was not drained from my Midwestern kin, however, but simmered just under their skin. When a reliable custodian for the farm could be procured, my father would pack the truck and drive us all to the far north of Canada and camp by some deserted body of water. Once there, we would fish for delicious walleye and fierce pike. I was especially thrilled by the occasional black bear glimpsed loping across the road in the beam of the pickup's headlights. The song of the loon still echoes through my memories. To get within ten feet of a moose swimming across a glassy-calm lake was astonishing. I loved wildlife and the primordial environment in which it dwelled.

If I had been born a hundred years earlier, surely I would have been lured toward the setting sun by tales of mountain men and buffalo herds, but reality slowly supplanted my reveries in the Ohio of the 1970s. I executed ambitious high school, then college, curricula, culminating in acceptance to medical school. Somewhere in that fast-paced period, Nature got misplaced. Subsisting in the city was a procession of parties, Friday night happy hours, sporting events, and study groups; golf and running were the closest I got to wilderness. Internal tension slowly swelled imperceptibly.

At the end of my second year in medical school an indelible experience redirected my life. At 3 a.m. on a dark, starry May night, I was walking through the neighborhood trying to unwind after a full, grueling day of study. My mind was churning with self-doubt. Could I succeed at this rigorous and expected pace? What if I failed in these endeavors? Suddenly the answers revealed themselves as brusquely as if someone had struck me square in the face. Stopping dead in my tracks, I gazed up at the brilliant Milky Way and inhaled deeply of the crisp night air filled with revelation; no matter what happened in school, the real world would always surround me. Each spring the maple trees would shroud themselves in tender, green leaves; roses would continue to beget their aromatic petals; snow geese would ebb and flow with the tide of the seasons. The fiery globe of the sun would rise every dawn, and then sink with the twilight into the western horizon. My petty problems were insignificant. The solution to my self-reproach was to become intimately reacquainted with the great outdoors.

From that moment on I dedicated my spare time to cultivating my relationship with Nature, with every weekend spent exploring a different trail or wildlife sanctuary. Then one day I stopped at a yard sale whose advertisements promised outdoor recreation gear, and two of the items they were displaying were an ancient bright orange Boy Scout backpack and a matching tube tent. I snatched them up for a few bucks, with the intention that from now on, instead of staying in a roadside campground, I would leave civilization behind and slumber deep in the wildlands; childhood fantasies were reawakened.

I convinced a college buddy to accompany me to a northern Pennsylvania forest trail, and though it was hardly wilderness compared to the grand scale of the West, nonetheless I worried about encountering a black bear. My initial attempt at bear bagging was a poor facsimile of the example in the handbook, but in retrospect it was hardly necessary. Also, for the first time, I confronted my fear of the darkness, far away from the contrived security of my car and human civilization.

After medical school graduation, I was elated to move to Missouri for the purpose of completing residency training. I was actually west of the Mississippi River! The city of Columbia is located in Boone County, which was named in honor of Daniel Boone, and I tried to envision the land as it was in 1788, when the famous frontiersman abandoned the settlements of Kentucky for the relatively untouched (by white man's hand) Missouri. Maps of the state promised residual pockets of wilderness to probe—especially in the Ozarks to the south.

At an outdoor recreation convention, I bought my first real backpack—a sturdy, external-frame rucksack that I continue to use for brief excursions to this day. Weekends were spent roaming the oak forests, ancient mountains, bluffs, and glades of Missouri and Arkansas. At Bell Mountain you can watch both sunset and sunrise without budging from the door of your tent. In the Irish Wilderness there are remote, awesome caves festooned with stalagmites, stalactites, and side chambers through which to meander. Abundant wild turkeys left their scratching in the dirt, their calls floating in the air to be heard from your bivouac astraddle a narrow, rocky ledge in the Paddy Creek Wilderness.

Initially I was a solitary wanderer, out to confront my fears of the dark, the boogeyman, and the wildlife. Though black bears reportedly survived there, I never saw them, and in fact the plentiful ticks were the most dreaded wildlife. Later, it was a pleasure to share my discoveries with close friends, and perhaps my enthusiasm rubbed off on them, as most have subsequently developed their own passion for backpacking.

When it came time to choose a location to set up medical practice, there was only one direction to look—the Wild West. One glance at the plethora of wilderness areas in Southern Oregon made my decision easy, and I followed the back roads of the historic Oregon Trail to my new home. Once there, I put all my possessions into storage and hiked four hundred odd miles over five weeks across Oregon on the Pacific Crest National Scenic Trail. By the end of the voyage my body and mind were totally relaxed and vitally enriched, and I was in love with extended wilderness trips.

Experience increased my confidence with basic survival skills, but the remoteness of the western wilderness takes some getting used to. Yes the Pacific Crest Trail is the well-marked interstate of trails, but there are no easy escape routes if catastrophe strikes. Self-reliance is mandatory here, as external assistance may be long in coming. Nonetheless, it wasn't long before I got gutsy and started bushwhacking by map and compass through the hinterland.

Time and experience refined my skills and the trips became less of an experimental struggle, and more of a rewarding bond with Nature. A mental checklist outlines what gear will be necessary to take for each specific location, season of the year, and length of the excursion. I no longer fret about preparing food, locating water, or finding an appropriate campsite. I have encountered bears, and survived unscathed. Each foray is a physical challenge and, most of all, a mental release from the work world. I have had the privilege of observing caribou herds in the Arctic Wildlife Refuge, black bears galore in the Marble Mountains, desert bighorn sheep at close range in the Gila Wilderness of New Mexico, and meteor showers in the rarefied air of the high Sierra. My yearning for the wilderness is more than a longing for the wondrous sights; foremost, the attraction is based on something more difficult to explain—especially to my mother, who has no conception of why I go to the woods. There are no specific goals to achieve, and no bell to ring at the end of the trail to signal victory. Most of all, a fulfilling backpacking trip is not a race from campsite to campsite; the journey itself is the retribution, observation and flexibility the methods.

Patrick is a diligent college student, with a tremendously empathetic heart, who grew up in Oregon. Typical of native Oregonians, camping trips to the rugged coast and conifer-hemmed Cascade lakes were an inherent rite of passage. As hiking trails are readily accessible from most campgrounds, he regularly hiked, as a social activity with friends and family, and had even considered spending a night in the backcountry, but never did until we met. I was merely the catalyst that prompted him to actuate that wilderness dream.

When we first met, Patrick was a light smoker, so that our first hike together, to the Sky High Lakes in the Marble Mountain Wilderness Area, was a noteworthy jaunt. The initial two-thousand-foot ascent was tolerable on the trail, but when we blazed our own path up and over a steep ridge (as a shortcut into the Red Rock Valley) Patrick was sucking wind. Long before we crested the promontory he had sworn off cigarettes, because that was the only way he was going to survive a long hike, especially if he added a backpack to his burden. To his credit he ceased smoking, cold turkey, that day and has never resumed; his body responded favorably, and as his conditioning steadily improved, the rigors of the trail are now easily accommodated.

It was a privilege to accompany Patrick on his initial backpacking trip. That enjoyable trek through the Oregon Dunes Recreation Area was followed by outings to the rugged Kalmiopsis Wilderness, down the scenic Lower Rogue River Trail, scrambling off-trail in the Marble Mountains, and tromping along the snowline in the Rogue-Umpqua Divide Wilderness. Spring break this year was divided between Redwood National Park, where we drifted for three days along Redwood Creek (including a chest-deep wade across the nippy waters), and Olympic National Park. I can assure you that the Hoh River Trail in March is a damp, cold, and mentally challenging experience; and we were both thoroughly chilled to the bone. In contrast, this Memorial Day weekend was a hot, dry march through the rough Red Buttes Wilderness of Northern California.

Nonetheless, up to this point the longest stretch that Patrick had dwelled in the backcountry was three nights, but he was thirsting for more, pondering aloud about what it would be like to linger in the wilds for a week or more. I could not answer that question for him. Some people love the adventure more with each passing day, and others consider it an ordeal and count the days remaining until the trailhead is reached. How someone will respond is pure conjecture, as they will not know until they have actually done it; an extended backpacking trip is an inimitable beast. The obvious solution to Patrick's quandary was to actually do it—effectuate a trip of at least one-week duration. We opted for early September, due to its optimal weather, minimal crowds, and reconciliation with work and school schedules. The preceding sequence of events climax in Patrick's question, "Where should we go?"

Because it was only early June, we had ample opportunity to research, wonder, and anticipate. The first thing I did was to review my file about

Rainier (I clip articles from magazines about interesting places just in case I might someday go there), which included a *Backpacker* magazine article description: "...a fleeting bloom erupts against an alpine backdrop of blue sky, gray rock, and the brilliant white of lingering snow." The Smithsonian Guide to the Pacific Northwest remarked that Mount Rainier is probably the single most recognized icon of the Northwest—which is probably true. Every visit to the Barnes & Noble bookstore wasn't complete without scanning for any new books about Mount Rainier, especially pictorials. Mental snapshots were conjured up of bears frolicking in the meadows at Indian Bar, the wild-flower perfume at Indian Henry's, the alpine image cast upon Reflection Lake, and the anxious crossing of the swaying bridge high above Tacoma Creek.

The most informative book we discovered was *Discovering the Wonders of the Wonderland Trail*, written by Bette Filley. Patrick was particularly enthralled with that guidebook; I believe he perused it from cover to cover at least twice before we departed for the trailhead, and I am convinced he developed an intimate friendship with Bette. Nearly every day he would recite a different passage to me. "Hey, Dan, did you know that Mystic Lake was named by someone who thought the water was mysteriously whirl-ing." "There are more glaciers on Rainier than any other area in the lower forty-eight states." "Bette says that from Klapatche the sunset on Golden Lakes looks like city lights or 'shining golden coins, a distant beckoning treasure.'" Bette also had suggestions on which sites to camp at, depending on how fast you intended to hike the trail.

As August waned, we got more serious about the trip itinerary. We didn't just select the number of days required to complete the circuit and then follow the guidebook prescription for that length; instead, we scoured all available resources to elucidate as many details as possible about the individual campsites, and more importantly, the scenery touched upon dur-ing any certain day, in order to decide where to pitch our tent. Equally important was to be realistic about how fast and far we could stomp with heavy packs strapped on our backs. With some misgivings, we elected, perhaps foolishly, to forgo any food cache, and to have in our possession everything required to survive for two weeks in the wilderness when we abandoned the car at the trailhead. I had sailed through a similar stretch without resupplying while traversing Oregon on the Pacific Crest Trail, and I now figured, with the weight divided between two of us, it would be no problem. Silly me.

After much deliberation, this is how we envisioned the trip: laden with heavy packs, we will climb from Longmire up steep Rampart Ridge along the southwest corner of the volcano, then descend briefly before rising again to Devils Dream Camp; day one will be a distance of six miles—not too bad with a full load considering we will have all day to do it. From there the guidebook suggests hiking ten miles to Klapatche Park; however, I am not thrilled about concluding the day with a strenuous three-and-a-half mile ascent, bearing seventy pounds of gear; hence, the choice is made to stop after six and a half miles at South Puyallup Camp, after a day of leisurely exploring Emerald Ridge, the sweeping subalpine meadow of Indian Henry's Hunting Ground, and the Indiana Jones–esque adventure of clambering across the lofty South Tahoma Suspension Bridge. (Patrick is already anxious about that crossing.) Besides, the book notes that South Puyallup is "...one of the nicest forested backcountry camps."

The remote west side of the mountain will take another four days to negotiate, commencing with the unhurried approach to Klapatche Park and its wondrous sunset—we wouldn't dare hustle past that spectacle. Next will be an eight-mile course to Golden Lakes Campsite and its intriguing patrol cabin, where we will pause for two nights, affording us ample opportunity to reconnoiter the lakes and forest, allowing time for our legs to rest, and consuming the weight of another day of food out of the larder carried on our backs. Well rested, we will conclude the secluded western stretch by awakening at dawn and descending the six miles to the South Mowich River, before the glaciers have a chance to melt enough ice to inundate the bridge located there. After safely fording the waterway we will then climb 2,300 feet, in three and a half miles, to reach Mowich Lake, where Bette recommends we stay the night.

From Mowich Lake the official route is via Ipsut Pass to the Carbon River, but the old Wonderland Trail track through Spray Park is seductive. Subsequently, our strategy is to bypass Mowich Lake for the allure of Eagle's Roost Camp, from which Spray Park is only a mile away. Another plus is that the camp is situated near Spray Falls, which "...cascade almost 400 feet over an old andesite flow." In my mind I can picture us lounging by our tent, perched on a rocky cliff, listening to the thunder of the waterfall, and delighting in its spray misting over us.

By all descriptions the north slope of Rainier is a parade of flowery parks separated by deep, glacier-carved valleys. Our seventh day holds promises of subalpine and alpine landscapes within Spray and Seattle Parks: bears galloping through the meadows, a panorama of distant Cascade peaks, floral displays, and an awesome view of the rugged northern face of Rainier. Sufficient time will be allocated to drift along the numerous side trails, which according to Bette lead to "…tree islands, small lakes, or scenic picnic spots." After lingering in the rarefied alpine atmosphere, we will conclude a relatively short five-mile day by descending to Cataract Camp. The ensuing day's excursion will be a mile-and-a-half plummet to the Carbon River, where we will turn right and trace that waterway upstream to its origin from an active glacier, before arriving at Mystic Lake—whose name itself arouses curiosity. The subsequent campsite is more difficult to choose; we both agree that the thought of camping amid the auto traffic at Sunrise and White River Campground is unappealing, and we definitely do not want to race all the way to Summerland. Therefore, the subalpine campsite in Berkeley Park, located before Sunrise, is the logical option. Furthermore, if we lay over a day there, then we can then trek north, off the Wonderland Trail, to Grand Park, which the guidebook vows "…is astonishingly beautiful…the grassy plateau…is unlike any place on the Wonderland Trail… Spectacular!" How could we possibly pass that by?

From Berkeley Park we will round the northeast corner of the mountain and travel along the dry, eastern ridges that teem with wildlife. A challenging thirteen-mile ramble past Sunrise, then along the White River, and ultimately ascending the Fryingpan Creek Valley, will transport us to Summerland; spectacular glaciers, sheer crags, and a classic shelter are included. Patrick also quotes Bette as saying that "…nights are interesting here too. With the critters being so chummy, you never know what's going to snuggle up beside you." Elk, bears, marmots, and mountain goats may all be encountered. After basking in Summerland, we will stroll four and a half alpine miles to the stunning Indian Bar Shelter; known as the Wonderland Hilton, it reportedly has bunk beds, a large table, and a nonfunctional fireplace. Refreshed, and with buoyant packs, we will then leapfrog over ridge crests (spying for the fabled goat and elk herds) on our way to forested Nickel Creek. On our final dawn in the wilderness we will arise to strut thirteen triumphant miles past Reflection Lakes and back to our car at Longmire.

Images of the Wonderland Trail are crystallizing in my mind, but I know they are only fictional—prompted by the literary handiwork of others. I can't wait to see how it will appear through my own eyes.

Patrick and I understand that this won't be a promenade through the Elysian Fields, as backpacking is never an idyllic stroll through the verdant forest. The longer the expedition, the more planning that is required for all contingencies. After a few days of sweaty hiking, no tap water, too many dehydrated fruits and vegetables, instant oatmeal for breakfast, and stovetop stuffing for dinner, quite a few packers will run for the nearest exit.

However, it is not usually the physical misery that compels folks to concede, but the yearning for what, and whom, they are missing. After the second day of a twelve-day journey in the Arctic Wildlife Refuge, one fellow could think of nothing but his son back in Chicago, to the point that most of the time he hung around camp and played cards until the plane finally picked us up. On an eight-day trip in Olympic National Park, half our group sped hell-bent for their car after only four days, because they craved the city and couldn't abide another day without a shower.

Of course, on the other extreme, I have cherished memories of magical odysseys such as the one in the high Sierra, when most everyone jubilantly peak-bagged the nearest summit—even after a day of lugging their heavy packs—and then serenaded the stars with song, late into the nights; no one wanted to leave. After a nine-day circuit through the Three Sister Wilderness, a good friend of mine was reduced to tears for the beauty and feeling of inner peace that the experience had instilled in her.

Not everyone is cut out for long-distance backpacking. Where would Patrick fall on the continuum? I was cautiously optimistic that he would love it, but he knew that if he wasn't enjoying himself it would be okay to pull out. "Are you kidding? I can't wait to go," was his emphatic rejoinder to that advice.

Preparing for a two-week backpacking trip is not a spontaneous, flippant activity. There are the usual logistics of gathering food for breakfast, lunch, and dinner—don't take too much food (equals weight), but anticipate burning lots of calories that will need replaced. What is your body going to hunger for seven days from the car? Comfortable polypropylene shirts, warm fleece jackets, waterproof coats and pants, and field-ready boots are checked off the preparation list. A full-service first aid kit, an effective water filter, a dependable gas stove, and enlightening books are accounted for. (It is still amazing to me how much stuff can be shoehorned into a backpack.) Swiss army knife, camera, film, toilet paper, candle lantern, camp shoes, wildflower guide, playing cards, ace wrap, sunblock, baseball cap, Lexan cup, bowl, spoon. Check, check, check. Waterproof the tent. Oil the boots. Fill the fuel bottles. Check and double check.

Mount Rainier presents its own unique obstacles to take into consideration. For example, there is no shortcut, so you either complete the loop, turn about shortly after starting, or exit to the closest roadway and hitchhike back to your car. Should you cache food and where? The weather can be fickle, with snow even in July, so how well will your tent withstand a blizzard? In an attempt to prevent overcrowding at popular locations, Mount Rainier National Park has designated campsites with a finite number of tent pads; hence, you can't just walk until you get tired, and then set up your tent anywhere. (Even off-trail camping requires a permit.) The trick is to anticipate how fast you will hike, and which site seems most attractive, then pray that your choices won't already be filled up by the time you arrive at the Park Hiker Center. (You can't call ahead and make reservations like a hotel—we tried.) I am especially concerned about the first day, as most people embarking from Longmire will be camping at Devil's Dream, and to continue beyond that site, with a ponderous pack on your back, would be torture. Despite the few downsides, the upside potential for a memorable trip is very high, and our preparations generate a crescendo of enthusiastic anticipation.

By August 29 our packs are stuffed, arrangements have been made for a house and dog sitter, and coverage organized for work. We are ready! On a misty Friday afternoon we load the gear into the Jeep and wheel north on I-5.

On Our Way

Gaia…is no doting mother tolerant of misdemeanors, nor is she some fragile and delicate damsel in danger from brutal mankind. She is stern and tough, always keeping the world warm and comfortable for those who obey the rules, but ruthless in her destruction of those who transgress.

JAMES LOVELOCK, *THE AGES OF GAIA*

Arriving at Mount Rainier National Park in the pitch-blackness of a cloudy night heightens my anticipation, like waiting for a curtain to be thrown off to reveal the prize concealed beneath. With the moon lost above the mist, the only clues to the grandiosity of the landscape around me are glimpsed in the narrow beam of the headlights. Broad, gray, furrowed trunks of fir trees rise into the darkness. The balance of the portrait is fabricated by my imagination.

Spanish and Russian ships plied the waters off the northwest coast of North America for decades, within sight of the great mountain, but the first documented observation was by an Englishman. On May 8, 1792, Admiral George Vancouver stood resolutely on the deck of His Britannic Majesty's sloop of war *Discovery*, sailing on Puget Sound, with his eyes set on a "…high, round mtn covered with snow." He then named the peak in honor of a friend, Admiral Peter Rainier. Rotund, myopic Rainier would never in his life come near the mighty volcano that bears his appellation, but, in a bit of satiric irony, the pronunciation of Rainier was reported by his descendants to be "Rainy-er." So perhaps the mountain was appropriately titled after all.

At 14,411 feet above sea level, Rainier is the loftiest Cascade volcano, and only Mount Shasta and Mount Adams are more massive. Its base sprawls over one hundred square miles, and it soars from three thousand feet in elevation at its base, up to the skyscraping summit in only seven miles—a stunning two miles overhead. Its precipitous slopes shoulder over twenty-five named, and numerous smaller unnamed, glaciers that, in aggregate, cover forty square miles and thus make it the largest glacier system in the lower forty-eight states. Five major rivers drain the mountain: Carbon, White, Cowlitz, Nisqually, and Puyallup, with all the waterways emptying into Puget Sound except the Cowlitz, which flows to the Columbia River. More than one hundred inches of precipitation falls here in an average year, fueling the force of erosion. In 1971 to 1972, the peak set a world record when an astonishing 1,122 inches of snow were dumped on Paradise. The abundant moisture nourishes a rare inland temperate rain forest along the Carbon River, in addition to the volcano's renowned alpine tundra.

Being a Cascade volcano, Mount Rainier holds hands in the great Pacific Ring of Fire. From its birth a million years ago to the present day, the mountain has had a turbulent existence—and it is not dormant. Though the last major eruption occurred approximately 2,200 years ago, minor outbursts continue, including fourteen in the nineteenth century. (A one-inch-thick layer of olive-gray pumice on the northeast portion of the park is estimated to have been deposited in 1843.) It is currently second only to Mount St. Helens for earthquake and volcanic activity. Rainier was formed only to be torn down then built again, and at its zenith it may have towered over 16,000 feet high.

The challenge of such a formidable natural obstacle proved irresistible to "western" conquerors. In the late afternoon of August 17, 1873, General Hazard Stevens and Philemon Van Trump became the first humans known to stand on the summit. Their fates would depend on the grace of the mountain, as they survived a frigid night at the top by huddling in a cave melted from the ice by a volcanic steam vent. A woman crowned the peak for the first time in 1890 when Fay Fuller did the honor. President Taft rode the first automobile to Paradise in 1911—the last two miles being pulled by horses through the mud. (His great weight came in handy, as the other lighter cars never made it.) In 1911 J. B. Flett and C. A. Barnes Jr. accomplished the first recorded circumnavigation of Rainier by foot. By 1915 the Wonderland Trail was completed.

With appreciation for the magnificence of the volcano came the realization that it needed to be protected. In 1846 the United States–British border was established at the forty-ninth parallel so that Rainier fell into US jurisdiction. President Harrison created the Pacific Forest Reserve in 1893, which President Cleveland subsequently changed to the Mount Rainier Reserve in 1897. It became the nation's fifth national park in 1899 with the pen stroke of President McKinley. E. S. Hall served as the park's first superintendent, and his 1910 vintage office is still standing near the Nisqually entrance gate.

Mount Rainier already had a rich and colorful Native American and pre-human history long before the European version was written. The present dome that natives called Tahoma (among various names) surged in fits and starts out of a swampy flatland. Ice age glaciers surrounded it, before relinquishing control to the verdant forest. Organisms of all shapes and sizes crawled along, tunneled under, swam through, or flew over its magnificence.

Furthermore, ours is not the first human quest to Rainier. Human cultures have relatively raced by, compared to the longevity of the volcano. In the present darkness, it is easy to imagine the sojourn of more desperate souls seeking the sustenance of a homeland.

Prior to the arrival of European interlopers this was the realm of the Nisqually. Tribal oral history describes how their Central American ancestors followed the receding glaciers northward into what is now the Great Basin. Eventually that area would become parched and infertile; consequently the band was propelled forward by necessity. Up and over the south flank of Tacoma, they emerged into an unoccupied Eden burgeoning with fish, game, berries, and grasses.

The abundant resources in their new abode must have astonished the weary travelers. Numerous strains of salmon, with year-round overlapping migration schedules, kept the streams glutted with readily available protein that would become the settlers' dietary staple; moreover, there were also deer and elk to hunt, shellfish to harvest, waterfowl to snare, and roots, bulbs, and berries to gather. The cedar trees yielded resilient wood for their houses and canoes; its bark excelled as clothing. Rushes and grasses were woven into enduring mats and essential baskets. It was clear to them that the source of this bounty was the great peak, which they reverently named "Nourishing Breasts" (Ta-co-bet).

What is most refreshing to me is their concept of naming plants, animals, mountains, and even themselves in context with their environment, in contrast to the conquering Europeans, who would assign the vanquished landmarks with titles from their foreign civilization. (Hence Rainier instead of Tacobet.) The river coursing through this quadrant was dubbed "Squalli," in reference to the tall grasses growing nearby. Because the waterway was the generous heart of the tribe—source of food, means of travel, water supply—they proudly proclaimed themselves the "people of the grass country, the people of the river," or in their tongue, "squalliabsch."

Not only did they not apply some Central American moniker ("New Guatemala" sounds absurd) to that worthy current and mold it to their desires, but, on the contrary, even their physique evolved into one with the environment. As generation begot generation, their trunks became husky, shoulders broadened, and extremities became less lanky so as to be proficient at paddling a canoe on the whitewater. The Nisqually identity—soul and body—was derived from the land. The country was not contorted by their ambitions. There were also other neighboring native tribes such as the Yakama, Cowlitz, Klickitat, Puyallup, Mashel, and Muckleshoot, who lived in harmony with the temperamental volcano.

To the Native Americans this great mountain was a source of water, food, and awe. Each tribe had a different but similar title for it: Tehoma, Takober, Takoman, Takhoma, Tahoma, and Tacobud; the middle symbol was always stressed because it signified water. The general concept of the sundry designations was also congruous. For some it represented any great white mountain, but the second syllable was prolonged when referring to Mount Rainier. To the Puyallup, Takhoma meant "breast of the milk-white waters"; to the Yakama, Tahoma was "rumbling like thunder near the skies."

Those who resided in its shadow also recounted legends about the origin of Rainier. The Puyallup story goes something like this: What was to become Mount Rainier was initially a beautiful maiden living east of Puget Sound. She married a young man from west of the sound, who already had one wife. The two wives did not get along and quarreled fiercely; therefore, with her son in tow, Rainier moved back to her homeland. The Great Changer was displeased and transformed Rainier into a mountain, with her son at her side as Little Tahoma, and her husband was turned into one of the mountain peaks in the Olympic Range.

In a consonant theme, the Nisqually version depicts the Olympic Mountains as once being people, with Tacobet residing on the west side of Puget Sound with the clan and betrothed to a young Olympic mountain warrior. They all continued to enlarge until the peninsula was very crowded, and so Tacobet decided to relocate to a less congested locale, free from competition for elbow room. She brought with her salmon and berries for the people. Without constraints, she expanded ever larger, and in the process consumed any person who happened to tread near her. The Changer was worried about the welfare of the people, so he played a trick on Rainier that caused her to burst into a harmless mountain.

The notion that mountains are sentient entities is pleasing to me. Perhaps if viewed at the accelerated velocity of time representing the perspective of the universe, the mountains would rise, quarrel, and migrate under the influence of the ever-changing status of the earth's crustal plates—just like a feuding family. The humanity of the myths is even more soul satisfying. A mountain is a kindred being, experiencing the travails of a birth, a life, and a death. She should be treated as a relative, not some inanimate pile of andesite lava and ice to be surmounted.

It is not the idyllic scenery that impels me to hike around this mountain, but more the sense of witnessing evolution. Several years ago I went to the Arctic Wildlife Refuge to behold the great hordes of caribou tramping across the unspoiled tundra (under the threat of oil exploration). There I discovered delicate alpine wildflowers underfoot, scattered wolves, grizzlies, and moose roaming restlessly; the soft hair of musk-oxen snagged in willow branches; jaegers angered by my proximity to their nests; and the good fortune of observing one prodigious caribou herd stretching out over the treeless terrain for more than a mile. (Even in Yellowstone that would seem absurd.) Such a spectacle could not coexist with man's infrastructure—the buffalo is evidence of that. So I was drawn irresistibly to the Far North to bear testimony to its grandeur before it is gone.

Now the Park Service is considering various development plans for Mount Rainier, and though I fear they will "open up" the backcountry to motorized traffic, my anxiousness to see Rainier is fueled by the concern that it will explode in its own inherent manner before I get there. Other than Mount St. Helens, it is the most likely Cascade volcano to erupt. That is neither good nor bad, but I want to examine the current landscape, to tread upon the soil, touch the old-growth forest, smell the floral air, and peer at the white dome of the mountain.

There is no doubt that Rainier will not remain in its current state forever, for the present is just a fine sliver in the time line. Artifacts attest that other people, other cultures, and other creatures have experienced a different Tahoma. Geologists have begun to decipher the turbulent history of the volcano, and do not conclude that it will abide as is. In 1992, top US volcanologists declared it the "decade volcano," and formulated a concerted scientific strategy of investigation. Of course, the fact that Seattle and Tacoma could be buried by a colossal mudflow in less than four hours arouses concern.

So I want to be a delayed witness to a dramatic geologic event. I was not present at Spirit Lake before Mount St. Helens burst; consequently I cannot clearly decipher the profoundness of the upheaval by evaluating the aftermath. Change is inevitable and should not be cursed. A thousand years from now visitors will ooh and ahh at the beauty of their era's Mount Rainier and Spirit Lake.

Ergo, I set out to explore the present park like one would trek Nepal before its culture becomes "westernized." Undoubtedly, travelers in future eons will vacation at historical sites of the obliterated western civilization, equivalent to how we now examine the Coliseum of Ancient Rome. We are not permanent, and the mountain is not a static fixture. So I do not want to be isolated in the here and now; starting tonight I want to intimately feel Rainier's past, present, and future all wrapped into one. Lupine growing on the volcanic ash in the path of a raging mudflow.

In the quiet of the night, reality and myth interact. The dark rounded hulks of the Cascade foothills step up to the mighty mountain. Icy, swift rivers run away from Rainier to the sea. Forest clear-cuts acknowledge that humans reap a bountiful harvest from the benevolent volcano. Hotels, bed-and-breakfast establishments, curio shops, and chain-saw sculptors all cash in on the behemoth.

Suddenly, the hands of man are cast off as we pass through a tremendous arch of cedar logs into the park. The ghost of Oscar Brown may still be collecting entrance fees in his cabin (circa 1908) on our right. Beyond the portal, the narrow ribbon of asphalt winds to and fro among massive tree trunks, fleetingly glimpsed like peeking at a herd of elephants with a penlight. The treetops rise into the darkness.

Longmire appears as an oasis of light in the pitch-black night, and at this late hour all is quiet. Patrick dashes into the National Park Inn, only to ascertain that there are no rooms available. Driving around the crescent parking lot, we can discern the Hiker/Climber Center in the dim yellowish glow of the street lamps. I had thought that there was a campground here, but Cougar Rock is actually the closest one; so we drive two winding miles uphill through the forest, listening to water raucously crash over boulders somewhere in the murkiness to our right.

By the Jeep's headlights, we set up the extra tent we brought along. (I have no intention of disrupting the backpack that was meticulously stuffed at home, and I'm not sure I could get all the gear back in again anyway.) My eyes rush to close so that when they next open, it will be to dawn's blush arousing the day for which we've planned for so long.

Longmire

A thing is right only when it tends to preserve the integrity, stability, and beauty of the community, and the community includes the soil, waters, flora, as well as people. It cannot be right, in the ecological sense, for a farmer to drain the last marsh, graze the last woods, or slash the last grove in his community, because in doing so he evicts a fauna, a flora, and a landscape whose membership in the community is older than his own, and is equally entitled to respect.

ALDO LEOPOLD, *THE RIVER OF THE MOTHER OF GOD & OTHER ESSAYS*

At last the eagerly awaited day is at hand. In the dull predawn light, we rapidly dismantle the tent and race back down the road to the Hiker's Center at Longmire. It was the roar of the Nisqually River that we heard last night, and the wide boulder-strewn streambed is now visible at the bottom of the steep cliff to our left. I marvel at the vertical, gray, rocky slopes of Eagle Peak rising across the waterway. When we next scrutinize the rugged crag it will be from the pathway hidden on its northern flank that leads back to Longmire—but I don't even want to contemplate the last leg of the trip right now. In the rearview mirror, snippets of alpine scenery present themselves as the heavy cumulus clouds, having dumped their wet bundle, begin to lift, unmasking the massive Rainier.

I am bursting with excitement as we swing into the curved parking lot across from the Hiker's Center, which is on our left, and the National Park Inn that is to our right. Between the two structures is an outbuilding with a public restroom, where we take advantage of the last running water we will see for a while and fill the water bottles, after brushing our teeth. The official trail clothes, boots, and socks are donned enthusiastically. Once the Jeep is secured, we spring over to the Hiker's Center to obtain our trip permit.

The Center is a handsome, two-story, boulder and log design, tucked away under tall western hemlock and Pacific silver fir. Stones, ranging from light gray to black, were used in the irregular patchwork masonry of the first-floor walls. The rough base contrasts with the dark wood beams that frame a row of second-floor windows and support the cedar shingle roof. The small maple tree in the front yard has not yet transformed into autumnal hues. Hustling past it and the prominent flagpole, we skip up the short, wide, stone steps onto a covered porch. Anxiousness allows no time to stop and admire the rustic structure, and, instead, we blow through the door in an impatient rush to get our wilderness permit. (As our attempts to receive one by phone and the Internet had failed, we are both worried that our carefully plotted itinerary will be dismantled. Hopefully the sites we chose are not already filled to capacity.)

Perched on a sturdy table is the centerpiece of the spacious room; a detailed three-dimensional model of Mount Rainier, five feet by five feet in size, hints of the land to follow—olive-green forest, indigo blue rivers, ashen rock, and milky glaciers. Thoroughly mesmerized, I glide around the table, tracing the dotted line up over crests and down through valleys— the Wonderland Trail. Animatedly I point with my finger; here is Devil's Dream, Klapatche Park, Golden Lakes, Eagles Roost, Mystic Lake, Sunrise, Summerland, and Indian Bar. I try to construct an image of each of them by synthesizing this mock-up with the guidebook descriptions. After consideration, I nod with satisfaction, as each site we have chosen still feels right. Our daily prescriptions of ups and downs, utterly apparent on this model, look daunting but doable.

The trail bounces through the multitude of valleys with a total climb of over twenty thousand feet, which is more than twice that required of the average summit climber. The Park Service advises one to "Be flexible. Be resilient" on this loop. I am sure it will be worth every difficult stride.

Plan in hand, I step over to the visitors' counter to request a permit. The ranger manning the desk appears to be in his late sixties, and is thin, well-tanned, and balding. Both he and his wife (who is helping a young couple decide where to stay in the backcountry of Indian Henry's Hunting Ground) are very helpful and friendly. After quizzing us about our back-country knowledge and experience, he sounds relieved and also convinced that we might actually know what we are getting ourselves into. Per pro-tocol, he reviews Rainier's wilderness rules: camp only in designated sites, haul out your garbage, etc. Then he pecks at the computer keyboard under the guidance of his wife, eventually coaxing it to the correct screen. Finally, "Okay. I've got you reserved for Devil's Dream, South Puyallup, Klapatche Park, two nights at Golden Lakes, then Eagles Roost, Cataract Valley, Mystic Lake, two nights at Berkeley Park, then Summerland, Indian Bar, and Nickel Creek. Is that right?" he asks matter-of-factly while tilting his head up to look for our confirmation.

"Yes. Great, we got them all!" I respond quickly with a broad smile on my face. Both Patrick and I are nodding our heads affirmatively. What a relief to have all the sites we had desired. The trip seems favorably destined.

After reviewing the computer screen the ranger clarifies, "All are indi-vidual sites, except for Summerland, where you have the group site." Again he peers up expectantly.

"That's okay," I assure him. By that time, one evening in the company of kindred spirits will be welcomed, though I hope I don't snore too loudly.

With our endorsement, he taps a key and the printer spits out our per-mit. After tearing it free he attaches a thin wire while reminding us, "You need to keep this with you at all times. Either on your pack, or if you're set up, then on your tent."

"I understand," I promise. "Thanks a lot." With a most genuine demeanor, both he and his wife wish us a good trip. They also reassure us that our Jeep will be fine left right where it is in the visitors' parking lot. I doubt anyone would want to steal the banged-up vehicle anyway.

Exuberantly charging back outside, I can feel the countdown reaching its exciting conclusion. Setting foot on the Wonderland Trail is now moments away. A last-minute equipment check reveals that Patrick needs gloves, and I forgot to bring a nylon rope for bear bagging and any emergencies that might arise. As we walk between the bathroom and the inn, my eye is attracted to a vine maple that is festively attired in a blaze of autumn red. We hasten by the wide veranda of the lodge and arrive at the general store only to discover that it doesn't open for another fifteen minutes.

The unanticipated delay redirects my focus to the physical surroundings for the first time today. Across the roadway, the deep emerald forest on Rampart Ridge rises toward the massive dome of Mount Rainier, which has fully shrugged off its opaque cloak. The volcano is enticing us, encouraging us to hurry.

Dan ready to go at Longmire

What would this landscape have looked like before the hand of man fell heavy upon it? The location's namesake, James Longmire, trooped through here in 1883 intent on climbing Rainier along with Van Trump, Bayley, and W. C. Ewing. At that time he was sixty-three years old and had already

24

been in the Washington Territory for thirty years, since piloting the first wagon train to cross the Cascade Mountains. His homestead was over at Yelm Prairie, from which he blazed a trail to the volcano in 1861. On the 1883 excursion he rode up from his home not as a guide, but as a mountaineer.

The intrepid group stopped at the home of Soo-to-lick—known as Indian Henry—and overnight persuaded the Native American to be their guide. Indian Henry convinced them not to depart from the Nisqually River, as all other adventurers had, but instead to follow that river to its source. The route was more than physically challenging; in addition they had to battle hordes of mosquitoes and biting flies that threatened to drain them of all their blood.

Realizing the passage for their horses would be impracticable beyond this point, they set up camp somewhere in the area across the river from the currently abandoned Longmire Campground. James hobbled his horses and stashed his gear under the watchful eye of Indian Henry. Understandably, the latter man assumed he would never see the quartet again; thereupon he moved the horses to better pasturage.

Perhaps it was to escape the constant stinging of the insects, but, to the surprise of Indian Henry, they all successfully reached the summit of Rainier and returned unscathed. Longmire corralled all his animals except for "Old Spot"; the equine was not where he had been hobbled. Following his tracks, they found the stray drinking from a spring that was laden with minerals. Being an enterprising businessman, James knew a good thing when he saw it, so he immediately filed a mining claim and vowed to return to this idyllic spot and build a hotel.

Of course this fertile valley had been a home for men long before James Longmire squared his first log. The Nisqually resided in three large villages in the vicinity: Mashel Prairie, near Elbe, and the third was ten to fifteen miles downstream from the present Longmire. A maximum of three longhouses provided shelter in each community. The cedar lodges measured fifty to one hundred feet long by thirty feet wide. Individual families had an assigned fire pit and sleeping quarters. (The latter were benches along the outside wall.) Indisputably, the dwellers roamed far and wide gathering Rainier's plentitude and offering thanks for the bounty. By the time James Longmire returned with his wife, Virinda, in 1884 to erect his resort, the Nisqually had been decimated by European diseases and confined on a reservation far downstream.

James realized that to reap any financial benefits, travelers somehow had to get to his legendary two-story, split-cedar hotel. So he carved out a navigable trail, factoring in a respite at the farm of Soo-to-lick (near present Eatonville) so as not to overtax his guests. Then a crude road, nicknamed the "Yelm Trail," was hacked through the forest by 1893 to encourage adventurers in search of Virinda's famous baked breads and huckleberry pie. In 1895 James slashed a road up the mountain to an expansive meadow, where his wife had exclaimed the first time she saw it, "Oh, it looks just like Paradise."

Such construction was most impressive for a pioneer who was seventy-five years old, but then again he was quite the go-getter. As John Muir noted, Longmire was "...a tall wiry, enterprising moneymaker, who hewed his way through the woods...He will do anything to earn money. He proclaims his goodwife as a cook, and says: 'Drink at these springs and they will do you good. Everyone's got medicine in 'em. A doctor said so, no matter what ails you.'"

There were forty-nine springs nearby, with water temperatures ranging from fifty to eighty-five degrees Fahrenheit. Those high in calcium and magnesium bicarbonates (sodas) attracted birds, and hence earned the label of "Pigeon Springs." Sodium chloride, sulfur, and iron predominated in others, such as "Iron Mike"; some of them can still be seen today along the "Trail of the Shadows."

James died in 1897, but the Longmire clan remained stalwarts about Rainier. His son, Elcaine, constructed a log cabin in 1888 that is the oldest manmade structure still standing in the park. (Elcaine Longmire's cabin and the site of the Longmire Springs Hotel are also along the Trail of the Shadows.) Elcaine and his wife, Martha, begot two sons, Len and Benjamin. The second boy left his mark in another way, by traversing the slopes of Rainier, applying whimsical names to streams, lakes, and other landmarks. I wonder if his penchant for the ridiculous represented playfulness or eccentricity. Ben's timing ensured that the amusing titles he assigned would persist, in all their perplexity, to the present day.

Neighbors came to the Longmire meadow in 1906 when the Tacoma Eastern Railroad built the National Park Inn. The new, three-story lodging was much fancier than Longmire's crude dwelling, with perks such as a wrap-around porch and fine handcrafted furniture. Both businesses profited when the roadway to Paradise (1911) and then the Wonderland Trail (1915) were routed to touch upon this piece of pioneer history.

However, Longmire's hotel burned down in 1920, and the park purchased the family's private land holdings for thirty thousand dollars in 1939. The railroad's lodge persisted, and in fact had already added a small cabin next door in 1911 to function as a clubhouse for entertaining guests. (That structure now serves as the gift shop we loiter in front of today.) The original National Park Inn also burned down, in 1926, but was soon rebuilt, and from its lengthy covered veranda one can gaze across the roadway to the meadow and lodgepole pines where the ashes of Longmire's enterprise are cast.

Finally the store opens. Inside is the usual assortment of T-shirts, animal figurines, plastic key chains, soda, and snacks, but they also stock the basic necessities for backpackers (not just beer and ice cream). We ferret out a pair of wool gloves, fifty feet of nylon rope, and a padded sheath for the candle lantern, and then practically sprint back to the car with our final provisions.

Patrick and I quickly and quietly prepare our packs. Oh my God...they do weigh a lot. Right now I'm wishing we had opted for one, or even two food caches, instead of hefting this bag of bricks. Did we allot ample time to plod deliberately in order to lessen the suffering? "Well here we go; it's time to find out," I answer my own question, as we help lift the packs onto each other's back. With camera placed on my chest strap for convenience and ice ax in hand for balance, I teeter beside Patrick across the parking lot to the sign marking the trailhead, located to the left of the Hiker/Climber Center.

We stop to admire the landmark and grin widely. The guidepost appears as solid as the mountain itself: a four-inch square, hollow, metal pillar that is painted Forest Service brown with a half-inch-thick aluminum plate bolted to its top. I run my fingers over the engraved message on the plaque:

**Wonderland Trail
Cougar Rock 1.6
Rampart Ridge 1.6
Paradise 5.7
Indian Henry's 6.2**

Your mysteries are about to be revealed. From out of the shadows of the dark forest, sword fern and salal peek with interest at whomever the next interlopers will be.

I snap a picture of this momentous occasion, concurrently with two cheerful, middle-aged couples pausing to chat with us. The two men have hiked most of the Wonderland Trail during three different trips, and the only remaining section necessary to complete the entire loop is the down-hill glide from Paradise to Longmire. One of the guys remarks that they could have sped through the final segment on their last journey here, but they wanted to savor the experience and not disrespect this corner of the mountain. All of us are bubbly, thrilled to be here on this beautiful day to begin our respective treks. Theirs is reaching its conclusion, while ours is just beginning.

Rampart Ridge

Climb the mountains and get their good tidings. Nature's peace will flow into you as sunshine flows into trees. The winds will blow their own freshness into you, and the storms their energy, while cares will drop off like autumn leaves.

EDWIN WAY TEALE, *THE WILDERNESS WORLD OF JOHN MUIR*

The initial footsteps into the cool woodland bring a separation from the realm of asphalt. With each stride, the noise of automobiles speeding down the highway becomes more distant, until they merge with, and subsequently are overpowered by, the music of the birds and the wind through the trees. I am always exhilarated to return to the embrace of Nature.

The forest seems a freshly watered garden today, after the evening rains. Ancient cedar and hemlock dominate the heavens, with diminutive deer ferns at their feet enveloping the pathway. Fallen giants create calm pools in the trickling trailside stream. With the ample supply of moisture and nutritious flesh of its mother, a new generation of hemlock is sprouting in abundance. Mushrooms of all forms and colors also prosper in the shadows. A dense underbrush of salal, devil's club, and salmonberry creates a playground for squirrels. Warblers sing their sweet songs hidden away in the treetops. This lowland forest is a thick, sweet blend of life.

I would like to say I am overwhelmed with bliss and well-being, but the truth be known, we are both sweating profusely within the first half mile. Rampart Ridge is not intended for the novice hiker. From Longmire, it is 1,200 feet upward to the crest, over approximately two miles. Obviously, with a light fanny pack that would be tolerable and even enjoyable, but the load of supplies on our backs resists the ascension. No wonder the guide-book so highly recommended caches instead of hefting two weeks' worth of gear from the get-go. Our first break is not long in coming. A perfect waist-level ledge allows us to sit down and take our packs off without having to lift them. I can tell from the look in his eye that Patrick is having similar doubts. Are we really going to be able to travel around the entire mountain? Secondly, what can I throw out of my pack? Lastly, why didn't I train more intensely?

The trail abandons the humid grotto and climbs more steeply though the thinning timber. Patrick takes the lead. Generally I prefer be in the "sweep" position at the back of the group; that allows me to frequently pause, examine the landscape, and photograph the flowers, wildlife, and trees without being a hindrance. Also, in that station, I can't fatigue fellow trekkers by progressively speeding up the pace, like I could if I was in front; I have always considered myself a strong hiker, with the endurance of a marathon runner. In years past, I would often volunteer to carry extra food or additional supplies to weigh down my pack, and hence keep me at a reasonable pace. These rationalizations all flash through my brain, while Patrick leaves me in the dust. It is apparent that on this trip he will be the stronger hiker.

It is a difficult notion for a competitive person to admit that they don't have the edge anymore. I will have to accomplish this circuit at my own pace, or risk not finishing it at all. I apprehend that reality, but I don't want to feel like I am hindering Patrick. This competitive, internal battle must be overcome so that I can stop and smell the flowers, without guilt. I must relinquish the desire to overly exert myself in an effort to keep pace with him. What is this crazy, Western-civilization, capitalist manifesto? The goal is to be first, to have more, to win! Right now I would settle for wind.

The landscape transforms into one of talus slopes and huckleberry bushes accented by western bleeding heart. Sweet and tart, the purplish huckleberries are a welcome treat and a good excuse for a respite. Eat a few berries, take a few steps, eat a few berries, on and on. Perhaps we will spy a bear sharing in this repast; I certainly hope we will have that honor, provided the bruin is not too near at hand or overly territorial. Out across the ravine, Eagle Peak raises its jagged crown. While munching on berries, we decipher the topo map in an attempt to clarify where the trail passes there. Two weeks from now we will be descending toward the trailhead in that dense thicket. What will it be like? What experiences will we have had? The anticipation of having so much time in the company of Mount Rainier diminishes the ever-present tension in my body.

The pitch of the hillside positions the treetops at our feet; otherwise I might have missed the pine white butterflies soaring resplendently. Effortlessly buoyant, they resemble fluffy snowflakes frolicking in the fir and cedar crowns. Perhaps this is their mating ritual or a just a good locale to have brunch. I would like to think that they are just enjoying the sunshine and reveling in the warmth of a beautiful day, at peace with all around them.

What is it like to be a butterfly? Would you salivate at the sweet aroma of hemlock, the fragrance of pine pitch, and the bouquet of Indian paintbrush, asters, and fireweed? Dreamily flitting here and there in search of nectar. Carefree! Can you be happy, feel glee at the sight of a compatriot, and lust for that special someone? Do you tremble when an unknown shadow passes overhead? Do the lyrics of the yellow warbler, that are so blissful to my ears, strike fear in your heart? As an arrogant species at the top of the food chain, it is difficult to put myself in your stead; perhaps it would be comparable to my living without shelter in the tundra home of the carnivorous brown bear, or having to swim for my supper on a daily basis in waters ruled by sharks. Do your experiences mimic the cartoon about the fish in the blender, feeling the tension of not knowing when it will be turned on? Or do you just accept your station and live each day in bliss, disregarding the pitfalls? Whatever happens, happens. I can only focus on what is in front of me now, and I will give it my complete attention.

A gentle breeze lifts the tree boughs and the butterflies ride along. It seems they should be cast about, like so many leaves, fallen from the security of their mother tree; yet they facilely float, and appear to take pleasure from the ride. I imagine my arms outstretched, capturing the wind, effortlessly turning and contorting my wings into just the right arrangement to plunge or rise or glide. This faculty is automatic and mindless, by virtue of my consummate focus on the meadow awash with blossoms below me. That aster looks delicious! The gales do not rip me asunder, as I can tuck my wings and allow the roar to go by; or perchance I have baffles that permit the gusts to blow through me. Up I go in the wisp of the wind.

The pack is as heavy as ever with each step up the trail, and I sorely wish I had wings. Despite my grounded restraints, my lumbering is distracted by musing about butterflies, and the ascent glides by. The regular rhythm of hiking always induces a trance-like mental state for me. Far from being mindless, I actually am more alive and sensate; in truth, this is one of the best attributes of backpacking. The humdrum of the everyday work world existence is cast away. I can perceive the cadence, and resonance, of my footsteps on mother earth. I remember that I have a sense of smell. The environment is much more than a field waiting to be harvested at my leisure, it has a life force of its own, which it unquestioningly shares with me. A plethora of animals, birds, plants, bacteria, and dirt that not only thrive together, but also depend on their coexistence. I am sincerely grateful that the natural kingdom upon this mountain can forgive my civilized sins, and welcome me into its embrace. I pray that I can be as kind in return. I want to be united with this sphere, and not the sovereign ruler.

The cool kiss of a fern grotto, the lift of a butterfly, the roar of the Nisqually River below, and a right turn onto Van Trump Park Trail bring us to the top of Rampart Ridge two hours later. Perhaps we can encircle this mountain after all! Of course, to celebrate our initial success, we immediately unburden our backs; there is nothing better than rewarding yourself after a vigorous climb with a gulp of water and a snack. My favorite gorp is a mix of strawberry-yogurt-covered pretzels, Craisins, and sesame sticks, though chocolate is always popular. We exalt in our initial triumph, with boyish grins plastered on our faces. "I can't believe we're actually here!" A quick glance at the map reveals that we have a lot to look forward to yet.

Pennsylvania Climber

Your plan to climb Takhoma is all foolish. No one can do it and live.... At first the way is easy, the task seems light. The broad snowfields over which I have hunted the mountain goat, offer an inviting path. But above them you will have to climb over steep rocks over-hanging deep gorges where a misstep would hurl you far down—down to certain death.... And if you should escape these perils and reach the great snowy dome, then a bitterly cold and furious tempest will sweep you off into space like a withered leaf....

SLUISKIN'S WARNING TO PHILEMON BEECHER VAN TRUMP AND
HAZARD STEVENS
BEFORE THEIR ASCENT OF MOUNT RAINIER IN 1870

Ten minutes is about the right amount of time for me to gulp down some water and a snack, and refresh my muscles without stiffening up—at least not too much. Patrick and I glance hesitantly at our packs, each of us waiting for the other to reinitiate the calf-burning march. My shirt is already soaked with sweat, and the chafing of the harness has reddened my hips and shoulders. Why does it always seem to itch at that spot between my shoulder blades that can't quite be scratched?

Just before I rock forward to strap on my pack, a day hiker strolls down the path from Longmire, extracting an indulgent sigh from me, as I now have an excuse for further delay. Tom, who is here from Pittsburgh on vacation to scale the peak, is about thirty years old, obviously in excellent physical condition, with chapped lips and sunburned face, and is adorned with stereotypical outdoor apparel: blue Capilene long underwear overlain with baggy khaki shorts, a matching navy polypropylene long-sleeve shirt, charcoal fleece vest and cap, large fanny pack, and a red-and-black Gore-Tex jacket wrapped around his waist. His attire is a far cry from what Van Trump and Stevens must have worn when they climbed Mount Rainier in 1870. (Afterwards, Van Trump reportedly advised would-be climbers to "wear a good set of woolen underwear.") Tom's clothes must have been slept in for at least one night, for they are crumpled and dirty. He appears equally bedraggled as his garb, considering he sports a week's worth of beard and unmanageable "hat hair."

Tom relates to us that for the last week he has been in the park, impatiently waiting to ascend Rainier, but the weather never cooperated. I feel sorry for his plight because it is not a nonchalant decision to scale such a mountain. He must have coordinated the details of his trip well in advance, including arrangements for a week off work, plane reservations, and obtaining a climbing permit. Unfortunately for him, optimal atmospheric conditions cannot be ordered. Instead of blue skies, he endured driving rain and dense fog for the entire week.

Over the last three months, whenever Patrick and I would chatter about our upcoming trip to Mount Rainier, most people instantly assumed we would be climbing it. Not only were they ignorant of the Wonderland Trail but they seemed stunned that someone would actually want to hike around the volcano's base for two solid weeks. As my mother would say, "What can you possibly do out there for that long?" Clambering up a sensational mountainside is certainly a more tangible endeavor, and is definitely more romantic. The goal is clear and easily dramatized: struggle to the top, conquer the icy cliffs, subdue the crevasse-laced glaciers, and then celebrate your hard-earned success. At least that is my image, though those who actually accomplish the feat likely have a different perspective.

To walk around the mountain is in keeping with my introspective soul. I want to experience the nuances of each valley. To differentiate the texture of the bark of a red cedar, hemlock, or Douglas fir under the caress of my fingertips. To be soothed by the earthy melody of my feet splashing through water, sucking out of mud, crunching across gravel, and thumping on solid rock. What aria does the wind sing as it whistles among the branches of a cedar? Happy yellow monkey-flowers will seek me out at every wet seep. My soul does not relish in the raising of my arms in exaltation when I have realized the apex of some palisade. In my humble manner, I search for my station in the universe, just another species coexisting with the multitude.

Most folks who chose to climb Mount Rainier start at Paradise, from which a steep, but not technical, trail steers you up to Camp Muir at ten thousand feet in elevation. (John Muir called this "Cloud Camp" when he stayed there on his way to the summit in 1888; fortunately for Muir it was not so cloudy then, as it has been for the last week now.) Following an abbreviated rest, summiteers begin their ascent at two o'clock in the morning, so as to be at the crest of the volcano shortly after dawn. In 1990 alone, 8,335 individuals sallied forth toward the summit, and 4,534 actually succeeded. In 1870 only two men consummated that coup, but then again they were the first humans ever known to do it.

General Hazard Stevens and Philemon Van Trump attained the summit of Rainier in the late afternoon of August 17, 1870. Stevens was the son of Washington's first territorial governor and was also a Civil War hero, decorated with the Congressional Medal of Honor. He found an enthusiastic accomplice in the humble mineworker, Van Trump. Philemon did not have any alpine experience, but he did possess a strong spirit and undeniable determination to see the summit, which is apparent in his excited comments. "...My first grand view of the mountain...impressed me so indescribably, enthused me so thoroughly, that I then and there vowed, almost with fervency, that I would someday stand upon its glorious summit, if that feat were possible to human effort and endurance."

An infinitely more accomplished member of the British Alpine Club—Edmund Thomas Coleman—joined forces in the assault on Rainier. It was James Longmire who guided them to the base of the mountain below the present Longmire, but he had no further advice to offer about the treacherous route ahead. Thereupon, the trio split up to locate a Klickitat Indian named Sluiskin, whom Longmire knew to be in the vicinity. Upon finding him Stevens wrote, "...discovery of a crude shelter formed of a few skins thrown over a framework of poles...tall slender Indian clad in buckskin shirt and leggings, with a striped woolen breech-clout, and a single head garniture...." After some coercion the Native American agreed to shepherd the group to above the tree line.

As the explorers continued to climb upward, Coleman became laggard and lost his pack before conceding that he couldn't keep up. He graciously gave the remaining duo his ice ax, which they thankfully accepted, and then, unencumbered with the straggler, made their way more rapidly to the tree line. It was there that their Indian guide made his dire warning.

It must have been a spine-tingling moment for the two fatigued but determined adventurers as they stared headlong across the ice, while trying to ignore their apocalyptic guide. I can almost envision them: woolen sock–clad feet stuffed into muddy, worn leather boots, woolen pants and long-sleeved coats layered over flannel underwear, sturdy wooden Alpenstock in hand, and the precious ice ax tied to a pack. They were resolute men, here to succeed, so up they went.

The course was initially easy, but then they required the use of the ax to hack footholds into the glacial ice above Gibraltar Cliff. To their chagrin, the day that had started out so pleasantly began to deteriorate, and they had to resort to crawling on their hands and knees to avoid being blown off the mountain by strong gales. Amazingly they reached "Peak Success" and defiantly raised their flags, then gave three exultant cheers that were swallowed up by the deafening wind. Yet, four hundred vertical feet still remained to negotiate to the very top.

I wonder if they were acquainted with Lieutenant Kautz, who had also advanced this far in 1857 only to retreat unfulfilled. Kautz had forged ahead when his companions had abandoned the quest, but not before the mountain had exacted its toll. Most of the company of four soldiers had lost fifteen to twenty pounds and would take months to recover. His Nisqually guide, Wah-pow-e-ty, was one of the last to concede, and stumbled off the slopes snow-blind.

Perhaps Van Trump and Stevens hesitated momentarily knowing their lives would be in peril, but then convinced themselves that they must reach the true peak. Blankets and heavy clothing had been forgone back at the camp in interest of speed; thus, at that fateful moment, they were ill prepared for the blast of frigid air that hit them at the moment they attained the summit. By then it was late in the afternoon, with storm clouds enveloping Rainier. Their minds befuddled, and their hands and feet numbed by the cold, a paralyzing terror must have swept through them—grasping that they had no chance of descending that day and were not equipped to survive the night atop the mountain.

Fortunately, fate lent a hand, or rather a nose. The intrepid climbers followed the smell of sulfur to a small cave melted in the ice by a steam vent. Their clumsy hands gathered stones to form a primitive shelter around the vent. There they huddled together in the wailing winds of the night, with one side scalded by steam and the other frozen by Arctic blasts.

At the cue of dawn's first light, they knew they would survive to tell their tale. Hurriedly scratching Coleman's name off the inscribed brass plate, brought to commemorate the occasion, they left the token on the mound of rocks that had been their salvation, then triumphantly descended to base camp at Sluiskin Falls. The falls' namesake greeted them boisterously, "Skookum tillicum! Skookum tumtum!" ("Strong men! Brave hearts!")

I wonder what it was like to be so close to the summit as menacing storm clouds crept overhead. A rational man may have relented and fled for safety. Nonetheless, they continued upward like metal to a magnet, rational thought be damned, their foolishness rewarded by the beneficent mountain. Today the escape route is much shorter, and a rescue much more feasible.

Tom was anchored to Paradise for most of the week, and in that time there was only one day when he chanced the climb up to Muir Camp. Weather reports had suggested that a break in the dreary pattern was possible, and he wanted to be ready for the final ascent if it did clear off. Disappointingly, with each step skyward the clouds inched downward, and by the early evening, unrelenting lightning flashed furiously and thunder rumbled with the mountain's fury. Hail pounded vehemently on the roof of the shelter in which Tom cowered.

The scenario brings to mind the local Native American myths about the evil spirits that lurk at the summit of Rainier. One version depicted "Whaquoddie," the giant Thunderbird, perched atop the mountain, but when hungry he would fly to the ocean to replenish himself. Sometimes he would gather up the waters and return cloaked with tremendous rain clouds, lightning flashing from his eyes and thunder booming from the flapping of his wings.

Whether driven by a low-pressure system, or the discretion of the Thunderbird, a mountain thunderstorm has a unique majesty. When I am out in one I feel the proximity of God. I well remember one occasion when I was overtaken by a fierce electrical storm while hiking on the Pacific

Crest Trail near Mount Hood. In the deepest forest there is no place to hide; one tree is as likely to be hit as another is. An instinctive panic triggered a search for any crevice large enough to secure myself, but none availed. I became cognizant that I was as apt to be struck while trying to hide as while walking, therefore I might as well keep moving.

Lightning flashed brightly enough to whitewash my vision, like a powerful camera bulb shocking my eyes, and thunder shook the ground, with its trembles coursing up through me. The tops of the hemlock and fir were being whipped about violently by the gale-force winds. At one point I brushed by a fifty-foot-high trailside snag that was burning at its top, with the wood crackling like a campfire and poker-hot embers showering to the ground.

Though one could go mad with fright at such moments, I instead felt an inner calm. If this were indeed my time to depart from this earthly domain, then it would happen; if it wasn't my time, then I would view the Columbia River in a few days. It was not a sad resignation to fate, but a sense of connection to the physical world. I was linked to Mother Earth in a very personal manner rarely perceived in the concrete arena of my everyday existence. Such insightful moments are to be treasured, not repulsed.

So Tom will have a memorable experience to recall to his friends and family back in Pittsburgh. As his consolation prize, the mountain rewarded him with one sunny day, which he could spend upon its shoulders, but not the summit. So here he is, day-hiking to Pyramid Peak, and tomorrow this Pennsylvania climber will be winging his way back home.

Fortunately Patrick and I are just starting our adventure, and, with a smug contentedness, I inhale deeply the fragrance and spirit of the wilderness, discharging off the yoke of civilization and returning to the company of Nature. Its essence pulses through me. My eyes are drawn overhead to behold the sky, which is now a brilliant, clear blue. Patrick is already fastening the waist belt of his pack, anxious to see what is awaiting us around this great mountain. I follow his lead.

On To Devil's Dream

*Give me odorous at sunrise a garden of beautiful flowers where I can walk
undisturb'd...*
*Give me to warble spontaneous songs recluse by myself, for my own ears
only,*
*Give me solitude, give me Nature, give me again O Nature your primal
sanities!*

WALT WHITMAN, *DRUM TAPS*

Patrick sets the pace as we head toward Kautz Creek. The next half mile
rambles pleasantly over gentle grades, allowing opportunity for me to
observe the surroundings with a more attentive eye. The forest is a thinned-
out assortment of Douglas fir, red cedar, and mountain hemlock that are of
only medium or smaller diameter, in contrast to the behemoths thriving on
the lower reaches of Rampart Ridge. Huckleberry bushes crowd into the
sunny gaps in the canopy.

The footing becomes precarious as the trail falls abruptly over the steep,
muddy bank of Kautz Creek, which is extra slippery because of the recent
rainfall. My heavy pack defies any precautions and shoves me in the back
when I least expect it, in its urgency to get to the bottom of the hill. I stride

with more confidence once the path spills out onto the level gravel bed of the waterway. The route weaves around many large boulders that are randomly strewn about. Nicks and gouges in their surface are silent witnesses to their turbulent journey, bouncing downstream in some past torrent to come to rest here.

The channel is not sterile, but, to the contrary, nourishes a diverse garden. Red alder that had been over thirty feet tall where perched in the relative safety of the upper bank grow as tangled shrubs here.

Pearly everlasting creates a green diversion from the monotony of brown and gray rocks. Protected by their rocky neighbors and exposed to abundant sunlight, they are only a foot tall when fully mature. While in the shadows of the north-facing embankment, their siblings are a leggy gregarious sort—hoisting their miniature bouquet of white flowers three feet above the ground. Here is living proof that the genetic makeup one is born with is not the sole determinant of the individual's outcome in life. Even flowers must respond to the demands of their environment. Every plant will emphasize those inherent characteristics that ensure their survival; perhaps human beings do the same. For the shadow cousin to wish for sunlight, or the exposed plant to pray for shade, is an exercise in futility. Each is equally beautiful. We can waste our entire lives desiring to be somewhere or someone else. I must always make a point of accepting my fundamental composition and maximizing its strengths. No regrets. No concessions.

Such are my musings as we proceed upstream through the brushy tangle, until the view opens up and a grand sight jolts my consciousness. Behold… Mount Rainier! Framed by an avenue of lanky hemlock and silver fir, Rainier soars above the valley to repose snugly in the warm, sapphire sky. Thin lenticular clouds stream up and over the summit, generating a thick downwind eastern tail. I bet those mountaineers lucky enough to have picked this day to "summit" are exalted by the magnificent panorama.

Pack and boots set aside, I walk barefoot across the coarse gravel to dip my feet in the milky white water of the stream. Fresh from its source, the fluid is refreshingly icy. I am fascinated by the creamy tint that testifies to the power of the glacier upstream, and I muse about how much rock was ground up to produce this coloration.

From this vantage point the violent history of this valley reads like a book. The vertical banks do not consist of solid rock or earth, but are a mixture of sand, stones, and boulders with a few tree trunks thrown in. Scrubby alder desperately cling to the loose amalgamation, but they will never become trees. A playful breeze tousles their scrawny limbs and stirs up dust from the unconstrained soil to blow across the rivulet.

Even the waterway seems transient. I have a feeling that the current three-foot-deep channel will not abide, but instead will squirm about in this wide bed, tossing and turning with the whims of the spring melt. As with all the canyons around Rainier, the Kautz Creek waterway is a dynamic artery; every month and year it brandishes a different expression. I wonder what it was like back in 1947 when the last major face-lift took place.

Small debris flows occur with regularity in the glacial valleys about Rainier. The steep mountainsides, frequent volcanic activity, and continual weakening of rock by steam and chemical-laden water foster instability. What starts out as a landslide turns into a runaway wall of wet concrete when the clay-rich material disaggregates and sucks up water. (The Indonesian term for such an event is a *lahar*.) They may also be launched from the mouth of a glacier when an outburst flood of water picks up sediment—often left behind by the receding glacier—as it races along the riverbed. As the thick mass roars down the canyon at ten to twenty miles per hour, the heavier sediment filters out, and eventually only a surge of water is left to play out.

What happened here on October 2, 1947, was anything but small. Heavy rains doused an already waterlogged landscape. A mile and a half upstream, the water sliced a channel into the Kautz Glacier all the way down to the bedrock. As the gap filled with liquid it created enough pressure to cause the collapse of more than a half mile of the glacier's terminus. A temporary dam of rock and ice in the narrow gorge could not resist the intense pressure for long, before unleashing an unrepentant rage. Fifty million cubic yards of debris with the consistency of wet concrete roared down the canyon, scouring everything in its path. The flow rumbled over nine miles downstream to bury the Nisqually Highway under twenty-eight feet of bouldery gravel. The present road, paved over top of the rubble, serves as a platform to view the Creek carving down into the debris and the ghost forest, which still stands testament to that dramatic day.

To read the post-mortem details of such a colossal event cannot possibly give flesh to the sheer terror that would surely overwhelm you when confronted by such a catastrophe. The angry Tahoma discharging her unremitting thunder! My mind is awash with fantasies portraying the sights and sounds of the mighty torrent…and I as the rugged outdoorsman overcoming all odds to survive the deluge. Movie rights to follow!

Our crossing of the creek is far less dramatic. A level tread has been planed from a foot-wide log to furnish a stable surface to lope across. As an added precaution, we unfasten our waist belts and shoulder straps, just in case we should carelessly fall the five feet into the stream. (The heavy packs would pull us right to the bottom, so they would need to be shrugged off easily.) Though it would undoubtedly be a cold dip, the water is actually shallow; accordingly I wouldn't have to swim through a raging current to safety, but merely stand up and shake off my pride as I stepped ashore.

Patrick crossing the log over Kautz Creek

On the far side of the bridge we rest upon a large trailside log and pull out the map to review the course ahead. This is also an outstanding roost from which to watch honeybees lunch on the bountiful fireweed; the brilliant chartreuse flowers sprout from five-foot-tall stems and brighten up a broad swatch of hillside. The honey sure would be a sweet treat if we had the time to track the bees to their hive, but a chunk of Hershey's chocolate will have to suffice.

Fully rested, we buckle up and embark on the climb promised by the topos. After rising twenty feet we crest the bank and enter a forest wet with springs seeping here and there. The abundant moisture nourishes the roots of thimbleberry briars, whose ripe, yellowish-orange, plump berries are bitterer than I had expected; black bears likely revel in this repast more than I do. Flat, bare patches of humus under the taller western hemlocks beckon us to pitch our tent and stay a while; however, smooth river rock, scarcely concealed by the forest duff, hint of a treacherous past. Tonight I want a good night's sleep and not star in some action adventure flick, so we stroll on by. Imagination is a good thing to take along on a backpack trip!

After a gradual upslope meander, we arrive at the first official trailside overnighter. Pyramid Creek Camp is located just before its namesake tributary. The rushing waters originate from the glacier sprawling upon the identically entitled peak north of us, which our new acquaintance, Tom, is heading for. The three individual campsites are reached by turning right and bounding up a few strides along a side trail through the huckleberry bushes. The clearings are connected to each other like pearls on a string, though the first site is the most appealing. It is a ten-foot-square plot of bare, brown earth that is level and surprisingly dry (considering the recent rain). A beam of sunlight slicing through the sparse tree cover highlights the serene patch.

Patrick and I take of advantage of the solar warmth and strip down to our shorts. Polypropylene shirts, by now soaking with sweat, are hung over the boughs of a young hemlock and are followed promptly by sticky, smelly socks. My body rapidly absorbs a pint of water and then demands some peppered beef jerky to replenish toiling muscles. So we are still carnivores after all! With thirst quenched and hunger appeased, I recline on my back, with my head on the pack and a baseball cap shielding my eyes, enjoying the sunshine.

Damn flies! They resemble miniature houseflies but pack a mean bite, supplanted by an insatiable itch. Though we should honor all creatures great and small, we quickly discover that they are easy to kill: they're kind of slow and land where you can get at them. If only there weren't so many of the relentless torturers. Our respite is aborted in haste, throwing on our sweaty gear and fleeing across the stream.

The ensuing quarter of a mile is damp and steamy, with water oozing from the ground supporting a quagmire of berry bushes. Soon enough, we turn right and head up an embankment that will not end until we reach camp over a mile from here.

Midday hiking in bright, balmy weather elicits a certain lassitude. Your legs move of their own accord. Your throat is somewhat raspy, pleading for water. Your mind is asking, Why am I doing this?

A welcome interlude of level ground on a bench beside a crystal-clear, cascading stream provides a mental respite, and then the trail switchbacks methodically upward, underneath the cover of towering hemlocks. The dense shade discourages undergrowth and therefore permits an unobscured view of the trail from the top to the bottom of the hillside. Glancing overhead, I notice that Patrick is a switchback or two ahead, and I hope to hear him cry out at any moment in victory, "We have reached the top!" I also dubiously scan for a shortcut, but the off-trail route looks even more formidable, certainly not worth the few strides saved. I catch sight of another group of backpackers down below, inching their way up the slope, just before the path contours north along the hillside toward the crossing of Fishers Hornpipe Creek. (So labeled by Ben Longmire, who thought "it sang a regular 'Fisher's Hornpipe' to us at our camp." Apparently that was a dance tune of his time.)

This is a very delightful locale to drink our fill and then top off the Nalgene bottles with the clear, cool water. The picturesque brook flows under the cover of the coniferous forest and is lined by huckleberry bushes that sweep away up the hill. A musty aroma permeates the air. Diminutive vine maples sporadically cling to the banks and drop their leaves to float away in conformance with Nature's scheme of recycling. As John Muir wrote in *John of the Mountains*, "One is continually reminded…of the infinite lavishness and fertility of Nature—inexhaustible abundance amid what seems like enormous waste. And yet when we look into any of her operations that lie within reach of our minds, we learn that no particle of her material is wasted or worn out. It is eternally flowing from use to use, beauty to yet higher beauty…."

I have a yearning to follow this current of energy to its source. Rambling through its corridor, I am appreciative of the lush garden it has infused with vitality. Water at its purest is the essence of life. Notwithstanding, it is easily tainted, poisoned to wreak havoc on the unfortunate thirsty animalia or herbaceous soul. There is no oil spill here, but is there Giardia? Casting aside thoughts of impurity, I envision this liquid pouring forth from some ancient and pure reservoir.

"This water sure is sweet," Patrick observes offhandedly.

By now the party trailing us has caught up, with a gangly young man adorned with stringy, blond hair, who appears to be about eighteen years old, leading the way. Close on his heels is a slightly shorter and younger boy with wavy, dark hair; his round, wire-rimmed glasses impart a more studious countenance. Another five yards back is a dark-haired, early pubescent boy who is a bit more timid. All three are clad in leather boots spattered with mud, hiking shorts, T-shirts drenched with perspiration, and either a raincoat or a fleece jacket lashed to their backpacks. Obviously they are not on a day hike.

The blond steps forward somewhat hesitantly as he greets us: "Hey, how's it going?"

"Great," Patrick and I chime in synchrony.

The first guy dips his head sheepishly, while pulling his water bottle out of the side compartment of his backpack. "Do you mind if we stop and get some water?" The second youth seems impatient with the permission seeking and is already taking his pack off.

Obviously we wouldn't deny them access to the stream, but I appreciate the courteous request. "No problem. Help yourself," I reply, simultaneously with the bespectacled youngster striding past the blond, water filter and bottles in hand. The third boy realizes that everything is okay and eagerly crouches down to help filter water, after dropping his baggage.

The elder brother is the only member of the trio who engages in conversation with Patrick and me. He is gregarious but initially shy. "How far are you guys goin'?" he queries with a nervous half-smile. "We're goin' all the way around. We started at Box Canyon, and stayed at Longmire last night, and tonight we're goin' to Devil's Dream." He is genuinely proud of their progress and I instantly like him. His siblings remain at a respectful distance, but are close enough to overhear the conversation, of which they are clearly interested.

"Yeah, we're hoping to do the whole trail in fourteen days," notes Patrick, who then confesses, "This is our first day, and we're heading to Devil's Dream too, so we'll probably see you there. It doesn't look far from here," he suggests with a glance at the map.

As we pour over the chart, the young man rejoins, "We're doin' it in nine days. After tonight we'll be at Klapatche, then Golden Lakes, then Mowich Lake." He counts them off with his fingers. Then his face brightens as he suddenly remembers something. "That's where we have a drop, and I hear they have showers there too. Man, I can't wait to clean off." All of us rub our wet shirts self-consciously.

"Really? Showers?" I am incredulous. How could Bette have neglected to include a statement about them in her guidebook? My expression is one of doubt, which the youngster discerns.

"Yeah," he assures us insistently, "and besides, that's our out if it's really nasty." I am uncertain if he is alluding to the weather or their body odor.

By now they are fidgety after having filled their water bottles; henceforth they sprightly throw on their packs and parade up the trail. The blond hesitates momentarily and twists his body to call back to us. "See ya at camp!"

"Later!" Patrick echoes.

Within a minute their twelve-year-old sister and brave mother catch up. "We're taking an easier pace. Hoping to see a little more," she says with a well-meaning touch of sarcasm. She stays to talk briefly, noting that this was a rare chance for the entire family to be together. She had gotten permission for the kids to miss the opening weeks of the school semester. So, here they are! Very ambitious and impressive, I think, as Patrick and I nod at each other in concordance. "Hope we didn't disturb you," she offers and then starts up the trail behind her daughter.

There are unwritten rules of etiquette among backpackers; but then again perhaps those of us who enjoy packing are of a similar temperament. The antithetical personality types are on top of Rainier today, boisterously backslapping, high-fiving, raising their hands high, and howling into the wind. Stimulated by adrenaline, that exuberant, talkative clique is already planning their celebration for the nearest saloon. In contrast, the average backpacker (myself included) is conscious of everyone's personal space. To be succinct, as a rule we are introverts. One of the sweet rewards of hiking around the mountain, instead of dashing to the top, is to have time to observe, contemplate, and internalize. Our toils are unnoticed. To some people they may even seem pointless, though nonetheless I find the effort expended is quite rewarded.

The family that just left could easily have converged on us with a non-stop interrogation as to the details of our lives, but they didn't want to pry. No doubt they are here to seek their own sanctuary, and personal space and privacy are reciprocally respected. I go to the mountains to break away from the masses. My mind seeks the quietude of a harmonic, unspoiled wilderness to rebalance itself, and I feel blessed that such places still exist.

"Come on. Last leg to camp," Patrick prods.

The concluding leg to camp is a reasonable, rising traverse across the heavily forested mountainside. Far below to my left are extensive thickets of huckleberry shrubs and maple trees. We scoot past the party of five, frolicking in a refreshing side stream, and then switchback right, up a moderate slope where we run smack into Devil's Dream Canyon. A cool mist wafts out of the forty-foot-deep, narrow chasm to bathe the moss and ferns clinging to the black stone walls. I peer tentatively straight down into the depths of the ravine for a few seconds, but impatience drives me forward.

On our right, Devil's Dream Creek parallels our brief ascent up the ridge until we enter Devil's Dream Camp. The unorthodox title was coined by none other than old Ben Longmire, who thought the stream was "...as crooked as a Devil's dream." The first three tent sites are beside the trail to our left, and are backed by a small glade that's supposed to be our water supply, but it appears to be a marsh devoid of clear pools. A short trail on the right leads farther uphill to campsites four, five, and six; campsite seven and the group camp are farther along the main trail.

After reviewing the attributes of each available spot, we select camp five, a minimally sloped site chiseled out of the hillside. Old-growth western hemlocks shroud the entire area, and game trails wander among the scattered rhododendrons and huckleberry bushes. The sun is approaching the treetops, leaving only an hour or two before darkness prevails. I glance to the east and wonder where the sun will rise over the prominent ridgeline tomorrow. Turning to face south, I recognize one of the luxuries of a developed campsite, situated just downhill: a toilet. Of course there is no roof, and only a pair of four-foot-tall walls separate my bare butt from the amusement of the tenants at camp four. Fortunately, it is beyond the reach of eyes and noses from our location, and, just as important, no one will shuffle through our space on the way to the john.

Next to dropping our packs, changing from boots to tennis shoes is paramount, followed quickly by dry shorts and shirts. Resplendent with our new duds, we retrace our path back to get water. Just beyond camp one, a de facto trail cuts left and makes a beeline for the creek. Once there our eyes are treated to the sight of water cascading off a ten-foot ledge into a calm, rocky basin. Canary yellow monkey-flowers, nestled among the rocks, smile with us. We scramble down the bank and join the adventurous mother and her youngest son, who are filtering water and also filling their pots for supper. Notes from the day's adventure are shared in calm, reflective murmurs as if not to disturb the tranquility of the scene.

After returning to camp, we attend to the mundane tasks of life in the woods: setting up the tent, cooking dinner, and cleaning the dishes. Most dreaded of all is bear bagging. I should clarify that there is a bear pole over by the main trail, but it hardly seems high enough to keep the bruins hungry. So instead, I tie the food bags to some nylon cord and string them between adequately separated, sloping hemlock boughs. It sounds easy enough, but the bundles are so heavy that I can't pull them up; hence I cajole Patrick into helping heave them up with his hands by pushing with a long stick, while I tug hard on the rope.

Feat accomplished, we retire to discuss the events of today and anticipate the morrow.

Tahoma Bridge

I went to the woods because I wished to live deliberately, to front only the essential facts of life, and see if I could not learn what it had to teach, and not, when I came to die, discover that I had not lived.

HENRY DAVID THOREAU, *WALDEN*

Awakening the first morning in the bosom of the wilderness bestows a sense of liberty and elation, especially knowing there are twelve such mornings to follow. With a lengthy yawn and stretch of my extremities, I rise to greet the sun. The aggregate tension in my face is released; the creases smooth into an easy smile. Today there will be no traffic, industrial fumes, incandescent lights, television, blaring horns, or noisy crowds. Nothing to anticipate but glorious meadows, rushing streams, and a rainbow of wildflowers, I muse to myself happily.

Between spoonfuls of oatmeal and sips of freshly brewed coffee, Patrick and I discuss the coming day. Indian Henry's Hunting Ground and Emerald Ridge sound spectacular, but it is what links those two parks that Patrick is anxious about—the suspension bridge across Tahoma Creek. The guidebook notes that "Tahoma Creek will be crossed via the highest, longest, and strongest bridge on the Wonderland. It is 250 feet long and 100 feet above the creek." As is often said, you cross each bridge when you get to it, no use fretting now.

As we are not striving to reach Klapatche Park today—like most others here appear to be—we go about breaking camp at a leisurely pace, which is just as well, because I am having trouble figuring out how I got all this stuff into my pack the first time. Finally laden, we stroll through deserted campsite number six and link up with the main trail near camp seven, where a doe and her twin fawns are cruising in search of salt licks. (Spots where somebody likely urinated last night.) Delightful?!

In less than a half mile we enter a true wonderland. Stretching before us are a succession of flower-strewn meadows, copses of subalpine fir, and the rise of Pyramid Peak fronting the towering Rainier massif. I reflexively cast aside my pack to better savor the beauty of the morning dew sparkling on a field of violaceous broadleaf lupine. They sweep around the waist-high subalpine firs in a royal carpet. Parent trees line the meadow, giving the appearance of a golf course, with a steep green hillside marking the far end of the fairway. A blissful sigh escapes me.

From here the path meanders from meadow to meadow, along crystalline streams and icy lakes. I linger in the vicinity of Squaw Lake to recall the history of this area. This broad diverse expanse is Indian Henry's Hunting Ground—a meadow that extends from Pyramid Peak to Mount Ararat. (Yes, Ben Longmire thought Noah's Ark came to rest here.)

One of the local tenants was Soo-to-lick, aka "Indian Henry," the Yakama Indian who guided Longmire and Muir to Mount Rainier. Muir described him as "a mild-looking smallish man with three wives, three fields, and horses, oats, wheat and vegetables." Indian Henry lived in the shadow of Tacoma during troubled times. Native American societies were ravished by diseases and squeezed out of their homelands by the white man's continued invasion. Some resisted, but others, like Soo-to-lick, strived to coexist peaceably. He departed from his warring brethren and moved to the Mashel Valley where he married a Nisqually woman from the Squaitz Village. By then the remnant bands of Nisqually people not already decimated by smallpox and measles epidemics had been transferred to their assigned reservation along Puget Sound. Hence, there was plenty of land available at Mashel Prairie to operate the farm, which he modeled after his white neighbors. When the turmoil peaked in the Indian War of 1855, Indian Henry fled with his family to this park, where he remained for several years until it was safe to come down. (He was eventually buried near the site of the longhouse at the junction of the Nisqually and Mashel Rivers.)

Mirroring their Nisqually ancestors, Soo-to-lick's wives picked huckleberries for jam or to dry and pound into pemmican, while they waited near Squaw Lake for their hunting husband. Their name for this bountiful meadow was Noachamuich, and it was the location of one of the many annual huckleberry camps established on the flanks of Rainier. In the summer and fall, small clusters of brush shelters would have dotted the prolific pastures of Paradise, Ricksecker Point, Reflection Lakes, Rampart Ridge, Mowich Lake, and Sunset. After the fruits were gathered, fires might be lit to burn off the competing trees and shrubs and encourage fresh grasslands, thus enticing deer and elk. Their existence here was not passive, but was an active partnership with the land and the other denizens of the wilderness. Triggered by early winter snowfall the band would drop to the rivers below in pursuit of salmon.

Remnant bands of Native Americans may still have been making the annual berry pilgrimage when George Hall and his wife Sue Longmire—Elcaine's daughter—erected a tent camp here in 1907. Located on the level ground on the north shore of Squaw Lake, the "Wigwam Hotel" rivaled Paradise in its desirability. In 1912 it cost seventy-five cents a night for a bed, or fifteen dollars a week for bed and board. None other than Van Trump regaled guests there with his climbing stories. I can imagine gentlemen and ladies of society sipping lemonade, while the summit pioneer described the fierce winds blowing across the dark, snowy dome. However, with the completion of the road to Paradise in 1915, few adventurers desired to hike the seven miles to Indian Henry's. In 1916 the Rainier National Park Company purchased the Wigwam Hotel, and in 1918 it was closed permanently.

Whispers from the festive resort mingle with those of the Nisqually gatherers to echo across the meadowland, wafting up the steadfast mountain. I trace the murmurings, until my eyes squint from the glare of South Tahoma Glacier, where thirty-two US Marines perished in 1946 in a plane crash. Their bodies were never recovered; subsequently the area was designated a memorial and is off limits. But even shrines are not immortal. The ice migrates five hundred feet per year, thus taking fifty years to travel from the summit to the glacier terminus. In 1982, fragments of the plane were exuded, but the men remain unaccounted for.

Farther along we catch sight of the only vestige of that bygone era, the 1915 vintage ranger patrol cabin. Tucked under a stand of mature subalpine firs, the rustic, simply designed structure invites exploration. It has one square room with a partial loft and a full-length, covered front porch from which to watch the wildlife cavort in the meadow. The cottage is constructed entirely of large, rounded logs cut to fit and is covered by cedar shakes. (It would have been sacrilegious to build this cabin with any element not native to this locale; the cabin is a part of the mountain.) In the backyard, a small, cold, brisk-running stream supplies water. Within the cabin is a pair of medium-sized backpacks, a red first aid kit, and the usual sundry of cooking, writing, reading, and lighting devises—of course there is no electricity.

The ranger station at Indian Henry's Hunting Ground

In the guestbook on the front porch, many passersby have left a message to entertain those who follow. Most passages are short and sweet: "Beautiful wildflowers"; "Awesome meadow"; "Still raining and I'm soaked." A few others are more expansive: "Still snow drifting up onto the cabin, must be 15' deep in places." All are signed, hometowns included. I write, "What an incredible wildflower display. Spring, summer, and fall all at the same time. Dan and Patrick. Oregon, 9-1-97."

Indeed, all of Indian Henry's Park is in a rush from birth, through adolescence, to procreation, and in death bearing the seeds of another generation. In the wake of a melting snowbank, avalanche lilies are sprouting, producing their droopy six-petal white flowers that fade to pink with age, and then are reduced to dark swollen grains, all transpiring within a few strides. On the cool north-oriented slopes, the furry green western pasque flower conceives its soft white blooms, while in the sunny meadow they have already been transformed into silvery plumed seed heads. The meadow is resplendently dressed in a variety of petals: amethyst lupine, golden groundsel, blue wandering daisies, white bistort flower clusters on leafless stems, and brilliant red paintbrush. In the boggy streamside, frogs, still dazed and sluggish from the long winter, hide among the marsh marigolds.

We wander along the cow path of a trail through the flowers, before turning right for a picturesque lunch at Mirror Lakes. Many people recognize Rainier from the famous postage stamp photo taken over these lakes by Asahel Curtis. Lunch is served amid the abundant flowers: yellow cinquefoil, puffs of white blossoms atop the green stalks of cow parsnip, which rise above paintbrush and lupine. Though warned about Giardia potentially infesting all waters, we cannot resist the urge to drink deeply the cold, clear water. After replenishing the water bottles, we pause to gaze at the mighty peak before returning to the main trail. The clear skies of the morning have given way to scattered clouds that seem attracted to Rainier. Glaciers drop in all directions from out of the billowing whiteness that engulfs the summit. Multiple ridges of dark gray, jagged rock partition the ice flows. Continuing downward, the pitch of the slope becomes less severe, thus allowing green terraces to abound for inspection at eye level. Where the glaciers bend around and fall over the hardened crust there are dark parallel lines of crevasses, which resemble frozen waves. Scintillating white ribbons stream away from the frosty masses to cascade down the mountainside in a series of cataracts. The ice, green plateaus, and hanging valleys all seem to dive off a cliff before us, and somewhere in the void between here and there is Tahoma Creek, which we will soon be crossing.

The sheerness of the gulf was not misinterpreted, for we plummet 1,300 quad-burning feet in two miles to Tahoma Creek. The Wonderland Trail is not subtle! Along the way the ecosystem changes from subalpine meadows, through silver fir forest, and ultimately old-growth western hemlock and Douglas fir to where the formidable bridge stretches over South Tacoma Creek. To Patrick this is another challenge to be addressed and overcome.

Suspended by cables strung between steel towers on either side of the gorge, the walkway is a 206-foot-long carpet of four-foot-wide planks. Now that might not seem very imposing, until you glimpse the roaring river far below through the gaps under your boots. The planks themselves are thin—not two-by-fours—and groan under the weight of my combined pack and body. Some are even loose, or cracked, adding to the Indiana Jones–like thrill. Patrick proceeds first, mincing his steps and grasping firmly onto the top of three, three-quarter-inch thick cables that function as a restraining fence. When he is halfway across, I boldly stride out, but quickly decelerate when the bridge surface starts rippling like a field of wheat in the wind. Patrick is yelling over his shoulder for me to stop, whereupon I quickly desist and wait for the bridge to cease bobbing up and down.

Patrick braves the Tahoma Bridge

While Kautz Creek had vague reminders of previous lahars, rugged Tahoma Creek appears to be regularly scoured. From 1986 through 1992, there were fifteen outburst floods released from South Tahoma Glacier, with at least one every year. The retreating glacier upstream leaves behind plenty of sediment to be scooped up by the surging water and hurtled downstream. These events usually occur during hot or rainy weather in summer or early autumn, "like now," I think to myself apprehensively. I try to imagine a bouldery snout, thirty to sixty feet high, charging toward me through this narrow canyon. Behind it a thick slurry of churning water, stones, trees, and mud creates a deafening roar that resounds along the precipitous valley walls. A strong wind would buffet my face, with the ground trembling under my feet, as a thick cloud of dust rises skyward, all hurtling toward me at ten to twenty miles per hour. With no way of out-running it, hopefully I would remember to sprint uphill, praying that a temporary dam wouldn't cause the mass to surge over the banks and cut through the trees after me.

Peering down now, I examine the frothing creek that is more than eighty feet below my feet. In 1986 it would have been only thirty feet down. It occurs to me that the gorge looks like it was fashioned by a giant ice cream scoop gouging away all in its path. Alder trees and Douglas firs clutch onto the rim, but nothing grows on the banks themselves. Fifteen feet beneath the exposed forest floor are tree trunks protruding from the gravel; boulders also toddle, biding their time until negligible erosion topples them into the turbulent river below. When was the catastrophe that buried that ancient forest under such an enormous pile of debris? What a powerful force of transmutation! Two miles farther downstream the Westside Road is permanently closed due to the danger. Along that road a former picnic area is being obliterated by bouldery deposits at a rate of one and a half feet per year.

Others have been here to witness the violence. "There are boulders as big as the entrance booth bouncing down the creek bed in a river of mud," a breathless wide-eyed tourist informed a ranger in 1986. Mud lines were reported to be twelve feet up on the trees around here. In 1987 a hiker was swamped knee-high in the muck, but was able to extricate himself. The guidebook advises, "Warning signs of an oncoming mudflow are: a mighty blast of air rushing down the canyon, thick dust clouds, violent ground vibration, the pungent smell of freshly killed vegetation, rapidly rising waters, a surge of oncoming debris, or sound like a rushing freight train… move out of the streambed and as far uphill as fast as your terrified little legs will carry you."

Our fording is much less harrowing, but nevertheless we take a break once we are on the far side. While we discuss the span, a solitary hiker struts resolutely across, and only halts after he is beyond us. Later, on our way by him, we interrupt his snack to say hello, before proceeding up the trail. A quarter mile later an unobstructed view of the bridge reveals how precarious it is—like a spider's web stretching over the abyss.

The continued ascent includes meeting a middle-aged couple dressed in their ranger uniforms, who patrol this side of the mountain. Half their time is spent at Indian Henry's and the other half at Golden Lakes. After exchanging greetings we continue up through the thinning forest and frequent avalanche chutes, under the constant harassment of biting flies. To our right Tahoma Creek roars through a rocky bed, devoid of vegetation due to its regular flooding. The silty liquid can be traced back to its mother glacier, now clearly visible on the west flanks of Rainier. A refreshing breeze hinders the pursuit of the insects, so we elect to pause and recuperate beside a bubbling spring.

While we survey the stark landscape, the solo hiker catches up with us again. Steve is a bit winded from the steady climb; therefore he rests for a moment with us. He is a twenty-something contractor from nearby Hood River, Oregon, with a confident demeanor. For the duration of our chat he persists upright, backpack in place, and arms folded across his chest. Yet he is affable and interested in the details of our excursion, and I ask him about his plans.

"Well I've got six days to finish the trail," he replies, with a trace of uncertainty.

My voice is tinged with astonishment. "Really? That's impressive. How many days have you done so far?" Whether he actually achieves his goal or not, it is still an admirable challenge.

"Oh, I only started today," he answers self-consciously, "at Longmire."

Patrick and I raise eyebrows; both of us are jealous, at first, of Steve's exploits, and then relieved that we didn't subscribe to that course. The furrow of his brow suggests that Patrick is puzzled, trying to figure out the itinerary one must commit to in order to finish the loop in six days. "How much farther are you going to go today?"

Steve rolls his eyes mildly and with a wry smile explains. "I had to pick North Puyallup, as Klapatche Park was filled up." (Oh, the pack from Devil's Dream got him.) "So far so good, but I'm not looking forward to the next climb." He sounds modest in implying that he might not make it there, when he is cognizant of his physical prowess. I am definitely impressed, but then frown imperceptibly when I realize we won't arrive at that address until the day after tomorrow.

"One foot in front of the other," Patrick cheers him on with a grin. Which is so true. I hearken back to my only marathon run, when it would hurt too much to consider the distance yet to negotiate to the finish line. Consciousness must be focused on each stride and the needs of your body at that given moment.

Steve chuckles. "Exactly!"

"So why so fast?" I good-humoredly tease him.

"I know," he smiles. "Crazy isn't it? I've only got until next Monday until I have to go back to work," insinuating that he wouldn't necessarily test himself so severely, but he has a deadline.

"Bummer," Patrick nods.

"Well, I can't complain since I've had three months off this summer. I already climbed Rainier and thought I would try to get around the mountain with what time I had left."

"That's ambitious," I state with emphasis, then add with curiosity, "What was it like up top?"

"Very nice," he affirms without hesitation. He subtly adjusts his stance to a more erect posture with his chest puffed out with pride, but not arrogantly. "But I was in Europe climbing most of the summer, so this wasn't that technical."

Well he has our attention now! Patrick perks up. "Where at in Europe?"

"Oh, Austria and Switzerland, mostly." The casual shrug of his shoulders is not convincing; it must have been a high point in his life.

Patrick is intrigued. "By yourself?"

"Yeah, but I met a lot of good people," Steve rushes to clarify, not wanting us to think he was a loner.

"Man, what a great summer," Patrick opines.

By now Steve is shifting from foot to foot and glancing up the trail, restless to push on. "Unfortunately it's coming to an end...well I better get going."

With that he is tromping up the gravelly ridge of the glacial moraine, aiming for the relatively open gap on Emerald Ridge. Patrick and I fill our bottles, simultaneously monitoring Steve's progress; only stubby wind-sculpted subalpine firs momentarily obscure his outline during the next first half mile, after which he disappears behind a mound of sand and gravel left behind by the retreating glacier.

I gulp some water and wipe the sweat off my brow. "Well that really is ambitious. I'm kinda jealous."

"Really?" Patrick isn't quite sure why I would feel that way and peers over at me for an explanation.

"Yeah, I just get this competitive urge to want to beat him around the mountain," I admit abashedly, then add reminiscently, "In the past I probably would have hiked the trail like him."

Patrick turns away to process this information, and hesitates before cautiously inquiring, "So do you want to go ahead?"

I laugh with the absurdity of the query. "No way! But in some ways it makes me feel like I'm getting older."

"Why?" He rejoins jovially.

"Well, in my younger days I was always the one passing other people. I took pride on breezing by them, and always tried not to look sweaty." Which is true. Hiking was a physical contest like a track event, and I abhorred being outrun. Life experience has since taught me that regaining the trailhead is not the proper goal.

"You still hike well," Patrick states with conviction, if not a hint of sympathy. Steve is long since out of sight.

"Not bad, but it is a little more of a struggle now than it was ten years ago. Of course I never carried a pack this heavy before either."

Patrick audibly groans as he stares at his black and gray, bulging external frame monster. "You said it!"

"But it's not so much thinking about getting older, it's more not wanting anyone to pass me." I am as much trying to resolve this internal angst as I am rationalizing it to Patrick.

"Do you really want to go that fast?" He persists with the accent on "really."

"No," I reply with conviction. "But don't you ever get competitive?"

This time it is I who peers at him expectantly. I understand that Patrick is not aggressive in the athletic sense, but the question is larger than that.

"Yeah, but not like that," he nods affirmatively and with a sincere expression accentuates, "I want to take my time, and take this all in. I don't want to feel like I'm rushing from camp to camp with no chance to stop and see things."

I feel defensive and want to make my point clear. "I want that too. Still it's hard for me to set aside competitive thoughts. When I think about it clearly it's silly. I love to look at the flowers and the wildlife, and take pictures."

"So don't think about it," he declares simply, but with strong sentiment.

The tone of the conversation is more somber than either of us had intended. I look over at Patrick as laughter wells up from inside of me. "I wasn't seriously going to suggest we hike that fast." With the emphasis on "seriously."

"Good. Are you ready to go already?" he jokes with a broad grin.

"Ready! It shouldn't be too far to the top of Emerald Ridge."

With the conclusion of that repartee, we reorient to the reality of trekking with a heavy weight on our backs. Knees strain with the rise from a full squat. Once vertical, we take another gulp of the cold spring water, and watch the afternoon clouds cluster around the summit, before gradually cranking our legs back into motion.

The trail enters a level, rocky expanse decorated with scattered, slender subalpine firs. Immature green cones sit atop their stiff short boughs. In the distance, lush green pastures angle up to collide with the thick frozen fingers of Tahoma Glacier; the dark snout of the ice field is less than a mile away. After looping around a huge knoll of gravel, I regain the profile of Steve, switchbacking up the final segment to the saddle.

What a typical "western civilization" concept, to aspire to be the first person to round the mountain. I chew that realization over in my mind as we start up the switchbacks. There is no winner here. I know in my heart that I will have far fewer regrets if I hike deliberately, enabling ample time for me to examine the surroundings—stop and smell the flowers, to borrow a cliché.

A longer pack trip requires partners of compatible temperament to make it truly enjoyable. I feel fortunate that Patrick did not encourage my racing spirit, but instead squelched it. More important was his acknowledgement that there is no right way. Perhaps we should pity Steve for the opportunities he will miss by marching so fast, but then again, some people hike for the exercise, and maybe even to revel in the body's torment of pushing to the edge of physical abilities. In that vein, observing the scenery would be secondary—just an incidental side effect. Our method is correct for us, and his is appropriate for him. The only wrong way would be if we ignored our inner voice and attempted to walk in someone else's boots instead of our own.

My feelings of inadequacy and jealousy are by-products of my workaday world. My need to rationalize supposed inadequacies is even more pathetic. I promise myself that I will not question my motivations, but will live each moment, however it presents itself, without worrying about how anyone else will think, or what schedule I need to maintain. That I could race around Rainier is as irrelevant as the belief that I could attain the summit; those paths will not evolve and satisfy my spirit. I yearn to intimately recognize the various moods of the great dome, imbibe of its primordial waters, and taste its sweet berries. This adventure will be focused on the sojourn itself and not the completion of the task. Everyone we meet is infatuated with how many days we are going to take to finish the circuit, like it is some contest. Getting back to the car first is not my objective; I would only be sore and unfulfilled. In some way I do feel sorry for Steve, because he will not witness the celebrated sunset at Klapatche Park, or linger abreast of a glacier at Emerald Ridge. Still, there is ample space on this mountain for our individual aspirations, and none is fundamentally more legitimate. The route of personal contentment is etched on an internal map that each of us must identify by honest self-examination—henceforth flows happiness.

A last steep switchback brings us to the crest of Emerald Ridge, where we are cautious not to stumble more than fifteen feet to the north, beyond which a cliff plunges two hundred feet onto an arm of the glacier. Tiptoeing close enough for a gander, I notice that it is mostly camouflaged by rust-colored rock, but occasional crevasses grant peeks at the steely blue ice within. Back in motion, the trail reverses itself to follow the grassy spine of the ridgetop westward. On the leeside, twisted thigh-high krummholz cower from the fierce winds, and around us is a dense bouquet rising above the knee-deep sedges. Chest-high green corn lilies look like miniature corn stalks, but have drooping tassels of dull yellow flowers; clusters of white flowers are held high by cow parsnips. The bright yellow of mountain arnica contrasts with pearly everlasting, paintbrush, and broadleaf lupine;

rose-purple petals surround the yellow hub of wandering daisies. Here I also spy elephant's head rearing up its delicate pink snouts. To complete this glorious garden are a few, scattered, light gray granite boulders.

Patrick and I linger on this bewitching prominence, and translate the visible features of the land into corresponding lines on the topo map. Straight ahead is the dense forest coating the South Puyallup River Valley. Tonight's campsite should be on the left (south) bank, and on the opposite shore is the daunting mountainside that we will ascend tomorrow. I am glad that we didn't decide to push on to Klapatche Camp tonight, and my legs ache for Steve, who has already rambled thirteen miles but will still have six miles left to go when he begins that climb in the waning evening light. Scanning up the ridge and continuing to our right (east), the trees subside and the green carpet of St. Andrews Park unfurls. Surely that is a haven for goats, elk, bear, and deer, but a meticulous inspection reveals that it is barren.

Spinning to my right, I discern the rock and ice flanking Rainier, then trace west-running Emerald Ridge until I am again aligned with the backbone that our path slithers down. In some locations the ridge crest is only two feet wide, with one side diving onto the glacier and the other toppling into a wooded ravine. A small company of day hikers wonders how much farther it is to the top, and are disappointed to hear that it is three-quarters of a mile yet to the saddle—sorry. Loose gravel hampers aggressive strides in the thickening forest. Soon enough we arrive at a tumbling brook where Steve is plopped on the ground refueling his body and regaining the will power to conquer the next ridge. Because we are so close to the camp, we only wish him good luck and then pass by without further ado.

The positive chi of South Puyallup is a pleasant surprise. We had expected an average forest camp, but instead there are five spacious sites nestled among the old-growth western hemlock. Vine maples comprise an understory, and huckleberry bushes, laden with ripe fruit, conceal the humusy earth. A tiny stream trickles past the campsites and down the gentle slope before cascading off a twenty-foot bank into the churning waters of South Puyallup River. Campsite number one must have once been the group camp, but a massive hemlock toppled into its midst, eliminating all but one good tent pad. Somebody cut three-foot diameter sections from the fallen giant to conveniently function as tables. We enthusiastically establish camp in this congenial glen.

The next priority is to stroll the requisite three hundred yards west on the South Puyallup Trail to the open-air outhouse. The white porcelain throne, perched atop its plywood base, is conspicuously foreign, planted here in the middle of this uncultivated thicket. A huge boulder at its backside acts as a disguise, the flat needles of the overhanging yew boughs serve as the roof; there are no walls. Patrick snickers, and insists that I must snap a picture of him on the commode, for the express purpose of showing his aunt the accommodations, because her "idea of primitive camping is Motel 6."

While waiting for my turn, I check out the Devil's Pipe Organ on the other side of the trail. This is a wall of fluted andesite columns over fifty feet high, with the individual six-sided flutes measuring about eight inches in diameter. The entire mountainside looks like it could be disassembled strip by strip, and maple and thimbleberry shrubs rooted in the cracks are attempting to do just that.

By the time we retreat to camp the other three individual sites have been claimed, including a solitary packer at number two. Lanky and gregarious, the forty-something fellow hails us from across the streamlet. Pleasantries exchanged, he explains that his family allows him to leave them behind in Chicago once every year so that he can backpack. The boundaries are clearly drawn, as he has a nonrefundable ticket for a return airplane ride ten days from now. His original game plan was to knock off the Longmire to Klapatche Park section today, but as Steve previously pointed out, all the sites are already claimed at the latter destination. Whereas Steve chose to slog onward, this chap opted for the shorter day. However, tomorrow he will hit the trail early enough to ensure that he secures a primo site at Golden Lakes.

After the usual swap of trip particulars is dispensed with, he is chomping at the bit to impart some important news from the outside world. "Did you hear about Princess Diana?"

One of the realities of an extended wilderness excursion is the forfeiture of your intrinsic community membership. While the preponderance of the world is glued to their televisions in a collective mourning, I am out here blissfully unaware of the event—at least until this chance encounter. It is always disconcerting to come back out into the "community" wondering whether the president was shot and World War III had erupted. Even mundane matters, such as two weeks' worth of sporting contests, will have happened without my knowledge of their results. It is an internal quandary to apprehend why I should agonize about global affairs in my everyday life. Perhaps it is the longing to be a member of an infinite commonwealth, or maybe just to have something to gossip about. Yet I am currently immersed in a whole wilderness to explore and consider. It is a wiser man that fully attends to his immediate surroundings, and a foolish one that flounders in the deluge of bureaucratic chatter.

Patrick and I sip hot herbal tea as we discuss the tragedy of Princess Diana and the triumph of our day. Vigorous, mystical Mount Rainier looms before us, and I resolve to pay attention. We cannot alter occurrences in London, but we can let each flower, stream, and mountain crest touch our souls. Petty jealousies and competitiveness must be thrust aside. The mountain must be appreciated as it presents itself, at the speed we are meant to hike it. There is no right or wrong way, only how it is destined to be for us. Extraneous emotions are easily discarded.

Now with interior fluids restored and exterior facade splashed with cleansing waters, I am revitalized, surprisingly not sore. Tonight I truly breathe deeply and sense relaxation's first flush within my body. A full day in the wilderness without machinery.

Klapatche Park

We are part of the earth and the earth is a part of us. The fragrant flowers are our sisters, the reindeer, the horse, the great eagle our brothers. The foamy crests of waves in the river, the sap of meadow flowers, the pony's sweat and the man's sweat is all one and the same race, our race.

CHIEF SEATTLE, *HOW CAN ONE SELL THE AIR?*

How gratifying it is to snuggle in a warm sleeping bag, listening to the forest awaken, with the smug knowledge that we only have three and a half miles to travel to Klapatche Park. The tracks of the crowd ahead of us have weathered a day, though our Chicago neighbor is determined to hunt them down. My reveries are disturbed by the muffled sounds of him hurriedly stowing his gear, followed by his quick rhythmic footsteps heading up the trail. I yawn luxuriantly, remaining in my comfortable cocoon while unzipping the tent door. A robin's cheerful call carries through the placid pre-dawn air. I purposefully had filled the coffeepot and placed it under the vestibule last night, so I can now percolate the day's first brew without even arising. The aroma of Colombian blend wafts with the steam to my nose. Absolutely sinful, I think with a grin.

By the time we have finished the first pot of coffee, the second campsite has also cleared. After savoring freshly baked blueberry muffins, we elect to break down camp ourselves. Tension perceptibly drains from my limbs with the absence of a morning rush hour. It always seems I am zooming from here to there without ever arriving, but today I am right where I want to be. Breathe in the coniferous-scented air; enjoy the trickle of dew from huckleberry bushes onto my legs. The river roars. Sunlight filters through the treetops. Soak it all in. Incorporate!

By now the third group has trooped west toward the road, but we, more fortunately, head east back up to the Wonderland Trail junction and turn north. I lean against the log handrail that protects the downstream side of the wide, sturdy bridge over South Puyallup River. The fifteen-foot-wide stream rushes by among the river rock, stirring a gentle breeze that massages my face. Alder trees and berry bushes create a dense, tangled underbrush, and pale yellow oak ferns hang onto the rocky bank beneath the bridge. Towering hemlock trees frame an unobstructed view of Mount Rainier upstream. The peak seems too distant to influence those things close to me, but, thrusting itself into the atmosphere, it forges an individual ecosystem—progenitor of water, protector of beings, nevertheless impermanent and lethal.

A persistent, well-graded climb through forest, then meadows filled with corn lily and lupine, leads us to the gateway of St. Andrews Park. At the crest, the view sweeps north past Mowich River and Carbon River as far as the eye can see. We turn east and skip along the ridgeline, with the knee-deep grass receding into a well-groomed yard filled with a stunning display of wildflowers. Tiger lilies seem to be bursting with happiness; their bright orange flowers leap and bound gleefully across the mountain, though they pause upon the advent of our arrival. I succumb to their influence with a giddy, childish step—positively happy. What a glorious day!

Sweeping north, the path traverses down a rocky slope amid small clusters of subalpine and silver fir. Two marmots startle us with their shrill whistles. The one uphill to our right takes cover, but the other lumbers up the trail a few feet then stands on his hind legs to shriek a warning again. They are known to sneak away with unguarded gorp, and they consider sweaty leather boots delectable to chew on, but I am not in the least bit frightened by his admonishment. Disregarding him, I scan the cirque to my left, where the west-flowing headwaters of St. Andrews Creek originate in the wetlands below me; surely there will be a bear or elk there, but alas, it is not to be. Instead, ravens floating on the rising currents and the scolding of Clark's nutcrackers summon my attention. Chickadees and juncos flit joyously among the treetops. I hardly notice the rigors of the brief, steep climb onto a small, rocky prominence, down which St. Andrews Lake resides in a picturesque bowl.

St. Andrews Lake is extraordinary. Patches of short grasses are overwhelmed by a dense carpet of red-and-white mountain heather, stunning crimson paintbrush, broadleaf lupine, and fluffy white bistort. Crevices in the white granite rock are stuffed with the white bells of heather adorning deep green foliage. To my right, a small lakeside depression contains drooping yellow glacier lilies, flowering in the recently relinquished ground of a melting patch of snow. Closer to the lake, Jeffrey shooting stars appear frozen in midflight. Across the lake the *eeenck* of a pika can be heard from among the talus—this is prime territory for them. A pair of ravens glides silently overhead, and then I hear the muted *whoosh-whoosh* as they flap their wings to maneuver through the firs. The lake's backdrop consists of subalpine fir and talus rising into the alpine high country all the way to the top of Rainier. The thin ribbon of a de facto trail winds up the mountain, starting from the opposite shore; the pathway is a siren call, luring me to come and explore, but disappears into the thick, white clouds that are descending upon us.

Patrick and I agree to separate and find our own spot to meditate in the early afternoon sun. I elect to explore the far shore of the lake and attempt to capture the many splendors on film. By following the western shore, stepping across the rocky outlet stream, and then skirting the northern bank, I enter a subalpine wonderland. The northeast slope corralling the lake is a rich tapestry of color—giant red paintbrush predominates, but there is also red-and-white heather, lupine, wandering asters, rosy lousewort, pearly everlasting, and the feathery seed head of pasque flowers to perfect the corsage. The cold, clear waters of the lake lap onto a peaty berm. Unladen, I float up the slope, passing through a small copse of subalpine fir and then crossing a small snowfield, beyond which is a sopping bog resplendent with marsh marigolds and glacier lilies.

Sitting on a dry, spongy mound of earth, my mind absorbs the world without interpretation…absently. However, my untrained brain cannot restrain its inner voice for very long. How would it feel to be a raindrop, pulled into a cloud to float along in the wind currents? Would I have a destination in mind?

Across the lake Patrick has abandoned his meditation post on the rocky peninsula and is currently unseen. I am alone to observe my friends in the clouds blowing up through the western valleys and skimming across the lake, accosting my ears with a light whirl of air. On the ridge thirty feet above me, the pair of ravens surveys the scene from the top of a fir tree. Their shiny blackness is swallowed and released by the billowing white cumulus fog. The view of the mountain becomes intermittent and then obscured by the thickening air. It is time to move on.

Only when I climb up and over the gentle prominence, do I spot Patrick lying prostate on the northeast corner of St. Andrews Lake. He doesn't even look up on my approach, as his attention is focused on something in the water.

"What are you doing?" My interest is piqued and I peer over his shoulder expecting to see fish or salamanders in the water, but nothing moves.

"You should drop down here and look. There's these bugs of some sort all over," he replies somewhat excitedly, but his focus remains on the bottom of the lake.

"Where? I don't see any bugs," somewhat doubtfully.

I appreciate his sincerity, but still feel a bit pretentious; I don't want to step right into a practical joke and look silly.

"They're all over. You've got to get down close." After a fleeting hesitation, I concede and set my camera aside so I can lie down on my stomach next to him. I had forgotten how secure it feels to be in full contact with the earth, like a warm embrace.

With the tip of his index finger on the surface of the water, Patrick is pointing at something in the water. What? I scan the water to no avail. "See…there." Below the dimple of his finger, something is crawling across a light gray rock. At first it looks like an inch of lake-bottom debris being rolled around with the waves, but its movements are purposeful. A small head and a pair of spindly dark legs protrude from the shell in the direction of its advance. Indeed, the lakebed is moving, under the direction of this small insect. It has welded together bits of wood, fir needles, and sand to form a protective cocoon; hardly appetizing for a bird or fish, which is the point, I suppose. How resourceful! "Oh. I see it now. What is it?"

"Well, I picked one up and pulled it open a little to see what was inside. It's like a small snail or something," Patrick confesses. Though most of us would not hesitate to impale a worm on a fishhook, for some reason, dismantling this insect feels blasphemous.

"Really?" I am not so much offended, as interested in the results. I peek over at him, anxious for the details.

"Yeah. I know I shouldn't bother them, but I had to see what they looked like. How they would react to me when I touched them. But then I felt so bad after I did it. It was like I disrupted its whole world." He sounds genuinely ashamed, and lapses into silence, absently gazing into the pool.

Part of me regards that notion as absurd, but I fathom the more profound truth, even still I attempt to comfort Patrick. "It's only a bug and there seems to be plenty around." Maybe yes, maybe no. The truth is that I have no idea whether this is some endangered species or is as common as the stones around us. My rationalization is weightless and floats away without impact.

A deer would not hesitate to eat the last blade of some rare grass if it was tasty; that's just the way it goes, for species come and go on planet Earth like the seasons. However, our human conscience knows better than the deer. We discern more than a hollow gullet, and the emptiness of our ecosystems is readily tangible; the futility of awaiting a phoenix is painful, as is the loneliness. Extinction is permanent. The immensity of it should stir all our souls.

"Yeah, I know. They're so minute compared to me, so vulnerable to my hands," he continues somewhat absently, not really addressing his comments to me as much as to the world in general. "I keep thinking about how miniature I am compared to the universe. I could be squashed like some bug, at the whim of some unknown giant."

"True, you never know," I agree, speaking to his reflection on the lake surface.

He continues softly. "The water is so clear, so peaceful. I feel bad to stir it up—like a violation. Even the sand and rocks seem to be resting where they are supposed to be. The best I can do is let them be." Our mirages in the water simultaneously nod in the affirmative. Man cannot "manage" the wilderness. Mankind can only hope to live within its boundaries, and in so doing inflict the least amount of harm.

We both vaguely monitor the progress of the water vagabonds, before flipping over and sitting with our backs against a short rock wall. Boots and socks are cast aside to allow our toes to dip transiently in the chilly liquid, quite refreshing to my hot, bundled, chafed, and sore feet. The sun rarely makes an appearance now, as the clouds thicken further and Rainier has long since been absent from our sight. Water laps across shore-side rocks and ripples thirty feet down the nearby outlet creek, before plunging over the westward-facing cliff. The cooling winds gust more steadily and urgently. Eyes closed, back against the rock, I soak it all in. I have a desire to plaster my body onto the ground, hugging the earth as fully as I can.

Several minutes flow by until Patrick's monotone voice breaks the silence. "You know, I feel like a little boy."

"Yeah?" I sneak a peek at him.

"Yeah," he continues more boisterously. "I was sitting on the rocks out there, and it was like all inhibitions were released. I was curious about everything and anything. Like I was seeing them for the first time: the water, the trees, the clouds. The lake is so clear, I just stared into it, which is how I saw the bugs."

"Curiosity is a virtue," I agree. There is more to inquisitiveness than just a desire for data; there is the implication that the object of interest has value; however miniscule, it is worthy of respect.

Patrick hesitates for a minute or so and then continues. "It was more than just being curious. It felt like the world was okay with me being here—despite playing with the bug—and wanted me to discovery its secrets. I felt so uninhibited. I didn't care if you or anyone else saw me face down on the water, playing with a bug. In fact, I was so full of wonder I just wanted to share that feeling," he concludes demonstratively. Patrick appears ready to cry due to a deep inner satisfaction. His heart is bursting and his mind is restless with compassion.

"I can appreciate that," I murmur.

"I knew you were doing your own thing, and you wouldn't feel slighted if I was doing mine," he points out.

"I know. It's cool." I am pleased, not jealous or mad, that he didn't yell out, requesting me to share his experience immediately.

"The other thing is that I feel so focused, fully attentive, like all my senses are coming alive. The bug was the only thing in my mind—no distractions, no fear. And I wasn't thinking about what I could do to the bug, but I wanted to see it for what it is. What an amazing thing!" He pauses and smiles genuinely, with head turned toward me. I can sense his internal satori, to be in the present and live the present fully. How fulfilling to stop the internal voice, stop analyzing, stop worrying about how others think, and replace all that anguish with quiet, peaceful observation. No further response is demanded or required.

High above the clouds, the sun is creeping across the late afternoon sky, and we become sufficiently chilled to warrant rising and donning fleece tops. The world is prompting us forward. Packs in place, we climb briefly before beginning the gentle descent toward Klapatche Park. Around the south then west flanks of Aurora Peak, we spot patches of red columbine, stonecrop, and broadleaf lupine before the trail turns north through a thin patch of twenty-foot high firs, after which we are treated to an elevated view of a sublime meadow.

Rainier rises over Aurora Lake in Klapatche Park

Klapatche Park is a fond reverie. To describe its physical attributes would not impress upon the reader how delightful the locale feels. Perhaps it would be different having to share it with the masses, but they are far ahead of us by now; this is solely our spectacular abode. Shallow Aurora Lake sits unpretentiously toward the west end of the flower-filled meadow, with a cluster of hemlock beyond its waters shielding the campsite. As we round the lake, a huge fallen giant, stripped of its bark, lies along the trail. The old-timer serves as the camp's front porch, a superb perch from which to observe the goings-on around here.

Sunlight peeks through the low-hanging cumulus clouds ascending from the western valleys to bathe tree-bound moss and lichen. A rock-lined pathway directs us to the encampment atop a small knoll, where a large level site, open to the breezes, becomes our domain. Expediently we shed our packs to explore the surroundings unencumbered: the old gray outhouse, the more than adequately high bear pole, and a well-trodden patch of dirt that is the viewpoint north. This spot is the same from which the guidebook describes incredible sunsets, with the day's last rays reflecting off distant Golden Lakes like city lights and golden pancakes. But, alas, clouds obscure our view. This was supposed to be one of the highlights of the entire trip, but not for us on this particular day. Strangely, my disappointment is transient. There is much close at hand to examine.

The absurdly comical edible fungus, otherwise known as the "chicken of the woods," appears to have rolled out of the forest duff ready to be basted and roasted, the size, color, and texture of a freshly plucked fryer. Aurora Lake is encircled by a ten-foot rim of mud created by the evaporation of the shallow pool. Grasses growing from its floor that stood erect a month earlier, are now bent on the surface.

Returning to our new home, the tent is erected, and then clothes are hung out to dry in the gentle breeze. Supper is prepared and eaten absentmindedly before we lean against a tree to sip a cup of hot chocolate. Such moments are soul-thrilling serenity.

In the cool mist of twilight, Patrick and I drift in our separate pursuits. I return to the front porch log to sit quietly and meditate upon the glories around me. In tomorrow's bright sunlight I will observe ground squirrels hunting for their meal of mushrooms, seeds, and the occasional morsel cast off by some human hand. Tonight, I am serenaded by the soft whistle of wind through hemlock tops, and the lapping of miniature waves on the shores of Aurora Lake. I am aware of my breathing, the pressure of my body onto the log and earth, and the soft crunching of the ground under my feet. I detect a hint of grass, mud, and fir in the air. In my workaday world, I would not believe that such senses existed, and experiencing them now is soothing, reassuring. Yes, I am alive! This is what it means to be alive!

In the shadows of my hearing there is a rhythmical whisper that announces the approach of another animal. Visibility is only thirty feet in the increasing fog, so I remain motionless and wait. Soon, a doe and a buck blacktail deer transform into reality, sauntering between the trail and lakeshore. Only my eyes shift to the right to monitor their approach. They are camp deer; without gunfire, and in the relative safety of this haven of humanity, they graze in peace. Surely they would spring away from a cougar or bear. Asynchronously they gracefully dip their heads and tear loose a mouthful of grass. Their large dark eyes warily scan the surroundings while they chew their meal. In their eyes are old, instinctual urges to flee from me and seek shelter in the tangled forest. Yet they slowly, placidly, edgily glide by. After ten minutes they are splashing through the water to my left and then disintegrate back into the mist. In those few moments, a cross-species rift was mended.

In many North American native cultures, humans and animals, indeed mountains, were once of equal footing, able to communicate and interact as a community. Usually by some human folly, that intimate communication was lost, but not the bond. *Homo sapiens* are but one thread enmeshed in the fabric of life. Not segregated or supreme, but united with the multitude. I feel so alive here. So sensate! Were the deer looking for some sign that I had bridged our interspecies chasm and become one with the world again?

When one ponders upon the large-scale interactions of Gaia, the breadth of the planet becomes evident. We marvel at the effects of El Niño causing deluges in the American Southwest and then are stunned to learn that the droughts in Southeast Asia, which curtail rice production and cause local starvation, are of the same etiology. As carbon dioxide builds up in the atmosphere, we blindly fiddle with schemes to combat the inevitable warming; a dash of iron in the ocean will allow algae to prosper; they in turn will consume the gas of concern, and hence cool the planet. But Earth also employs the winds to blow iron-rich dust off the arid plains to accomplish this same feat. We are astonished by the statistics showing significantly increased rainfall in the downwind shadow of pollution-laden cities. Could a few faithful humans kicking up dust in a frenzied dance accomplish the same result? We scoff and snicker at the absurdity of the native rain dance, yet are we stomping on Nature's cycles with impunity? Results as yet unknown?

Can we even begin to guess at how Mother Earth may be lamenting to the cosmos? Ninety percent of the mass of the universe is unaccounted for; dark matter, which is unseen and uncomprehended, fills the voids of space. Our Milky Way galaxy wears a huge halo of unseen matter that extends to the halos of our closest galactic neighbors. Maybe we are just some bright jewel embedded in the belt of the real universe, like a sequin on a black dress. Warm, flowing waters stir the winds, which blow the dust, which feed the algae, which eat the gases that we exhale from our humanity. How long will Nature clean up after us? Perhaps Mother Earth is screaming to the heavens, "Please, just one comet to cleanse me of this infestation." Only the arrogance of mankind makes that supposition sound ludicrous.

With the fascinating advances and discoveries of quantum physics, the line between concrete reality and spirituality is becoming blurrier. John Gribbin, in his book *Schrödinger's Kittens and the Search for Reality*, posed Schrödinger's theoretical cat-in-the-box experiment in an intriguing manner. Two identical kittens are placed in two different spaceships that are connected by a thin tube. An electron is injected into the tube, and the electron must enter one of the two craft (exactly a 50 percent chance for each ship). The rockets are sealed, without us ever knowing into which ship the electron actually went. Its ultimate destination is important, because when the electron enters a ship it will trigger a reaction that releases a toxic gas, and thus kills the inhabitant cat. (The tube was partitioned so the electron could only end up in one of the vessels and not bounce back and forth.) The question is, would the cat in the poisoned spacecraft die instantly if there weren't anyone there to confirm the outcome? It is kind of the "If a tree fell in the forest and no one was there, would it make a noise?" question.

To add to the drama, the spaceships would then be severed and shot into space in opposite directions, without so much as a peek. Common sense dictates that one cat is already dead and the other is alive and well, but scientific research (not with cats of course) suggests that is not the situation. Furthermore, it is suggested that only when some intelligent onlooker opens the door to evaluate the felines is the outcome actually determined. Observation makes it so. The electron can be in one of two places, and only at the critical moment of discovery does the electron decide at which of the two sites it actually is. The cats are suspended in limbo, destinies bound together, until someone opens the door; one is dead and the other is alive. If these experimental cats were ageless and survived until landing on some distant celestial body that held intelligent life, and those aliens opened the chamber, then and only then would the fates of the cats be sealed. To the cats it would seem instantaneous; time is just another dimension, after all. As Gribbin wrote, "as if each capsule contains two ghosts, representing alternative versions of history, one of which fades away while the other becomes real at the moment of observation...You could argue that the act of observation sends a signal not just across space but also echoing back across time, back to the moment when the electron was released, determining which capsule it went into." Pretty wild stuff! Perhaps there is something to the power of positive thinking after all.

We may have more influence over our world than we can even begin to comprehend. Shamans claim to transcend the physical world to interact in other dimensions, and, strangely, as physics advances it seems to blend into metaphysics. The native rain dance may do more than just kick up a little dust; perhaps there is magic in the chants that help the atmosphere choose between drought and rain. At a local Native American feast to honor the arrival of the spring salmon run, all present thanked the fish and the river it arrived in. Furthermore, enlightened and properly prepared kinsmen put the bones of a blessed fish back into the waters, so that he might return to his brethren in the ocean and report on how well treated he was here. Ridiculous, the western-trained mind might say, but in the following year there was a record return of salmon.

People are linked for eternity with all other living entities. Important outcomes may be lingering out there undetermined, waiting for our observance. In some cases we may be unaware of the question, but in other instances we may discern the effects of our actions. The human race is busy building diabolical machines to drop electrons in, like a fuse in a bomb. I am not contemplating the obvious—nuclear weapons—but the more abstruse: deforestation, pollution, over-population, and the ready spread of diseases around the globe by travelers, for example. Maybe we are the cats, locked in our own trap, waiting for some unknown external intelligence to observe us and decide our fate. Perhaps the Earth is performing its own cosmic rain dance.

Sorry, I didn't intend to be so pessimistic, especially sitting here in this incredible sanctuary. Mankind has done some things right, for instance designating Mount Rainier National Park. As a whole, humans are caring, but we must channel that goodwill toward our co-resident species. If we can be patient, perceptive, and receptive and avoid arrogance, perhaps we will talk with the animals again. Perhaps the deer can greet me as they saunter by, and I can point out some particularly good grasses for them. Perhaps Tahoma will call out a warning so that I may vacate the territory before it erupts. An absurd fantasy, but just maybe.

Golden Lakes

The land retains an identity of its own, still deeper and more subtle than
we can know. Our obligation toward it then becomes simple: to approach
with an uncalculating mind, with an attitude of regard…be alert for its
openings, for that moment when something sacred reveals itself within the
mundane, and you know the land knows you are there.

BARRY LOPEZ, ARCTIC DREAMS

The moon has burned away the clouds once again, revealing Rainier poised majestically upright in the brilliant morning light. From my vantage point on the front porch log, the snowy peak is reflected precisely on the calm waters of Aurora Lake. The shimmering mirror image bares the fact that the volcano's crown is not a smooth dome, but instead is a double hump. Beyond the opposite shore, knee-deep green grass highlighted by dew-bathed lupine bends sluggishly toward the distant woods, before all is lost over the precipitous embankment down which we will proceed later. Across the ravine is an ominous wall with vertical scars, resembling the claw marks of some giant beast clambering to extricate itself out of the blind chasm; the North Puyallup River is somewhere in that void. Across the shear valley, waterfalls cascade from the white bulk of the Puyallup

Glacier, and between the snowfields are small, emerald meadows, which provide the perfect refuge from predators for mountain goats; lamentably, no animals are visible on a thorough survey.

Closing my eyes, I relish the sun's warm rays upon my cheeks, and the sickening sweet fragrance of hemlock lingering in the air. My attention is drawn to the rotund ground squirrels playfully chasing each other behind me, though their antics are not a mere game, for the reason that each is intent on procuring the best foraging grounds. Their tiny feet and claws rapidly scratch, scratch while they run along the log then speed across turf and leap into the lower branches of a hemlock. One of them sits on his haunches, munching on a small dark mushroom. Their frolicking is a source of amusement for me, but to them it is a wrestling contest for survival, because the summer sun prepares only a transient feast to devour before the emaciating winter chill arrives. The sprightly creatures are not morose, however, but seem to revel in the moment.

Patrick's filtering of water from the shallow, muddy shore momentarily fragments the crystal-clear reflection of Rainier on the surface of Aurora Lake. We are excited to move on and see what the environs will reveal to us today. The accumulated stress of my habitual sphere is beginning to abate from my muscles and brain. (It usually requires a minimum of forty-eight hours immersed in wilderness for any substantial internal transformation to occur, and a week to metamorphose into and become attuned with the natural world of creation.) Similar to many folks in the Northwest, I often ask myself why I haven't pursued a career in the outdoors. Perhaps it would become too mundane, but, more likely than not, I have not transcended childhood expectations of worth.

After dismantling camp and restuffing the packs, Patrick and I glide through the meadow and then plunge over the headwall. The river is 1,700 feet below our present position, but we will reach it in less than three miles. I am sure Steve's legs were intensely burning by the time he arrived here two days ago, and then, with every bottomward footfall, his quadriceps must have quivered and threatened to concede control to gravity.

Shortly, we pass under a modest north-facing escarpment that seeps water from every nook and cranny. The downhill beneficiaries are salmonberry and thimbleberry bushes that form an impassable, chest-deep jungle. Where slippery acquiesces to dry footing, huckleberry bushes predominate. The second half of the descent switchbacks through old-growth Douglas fir, western hemlock, and a smattering of cedar trees, with ferns cloaking the ground. The trail's gradient becomes less severe, while crossing and recrossing a beautiful gurgling brook, before we stride onto the foreign hardness of asphalt on the abandoned West Side Road.

This byway has been closed for most of the 1990s because of a mud-flow at Tahoma Creek; there are no plans to reopen it. How surreal it is to appraise the decorative masonry of a scenic overlook intended for the eyes of car passengers. Echoes reverberate through the valley, of toddlers screeching their pleasure at chipmunks dancing on the stone walls for the price of a peanut; retired couples snapping a photograph from their Chevy pickup, trailer in tow. The revving of engines and the artificial breeze of a passing vehicle are gone. Now all is overgrown by grass and alder trees.

There is a westerly heading trail that takes advantage of the level roadbed, but, instead of autos, it is now only wide enough for horses. The American West is replete with discarded roads and forsaken hiking trails; it is always peculiar to chance upon their remnants. Mother Nature deliberately reconditions civilization's castoffs and restores them into the wilderness flock. Similar reclamations undoubtedly are occurring in the East, where Revolution-era farms are being transformed back into woodland. The leaning weathered gray skeleton of a barn is no longer the abode of milking cows and plow horses, but now is merely a scenic photo opportunity for metropolitan tourists. One dark, stormy night, a nor'easter will shake it asunder to the realm of worms and fungi, as the forest repossesses its lost timbers. Out here in the West, the earth reclaims whole towns.

History abounds with ghost towns and lost civilizations. Mankind can be an acerbic tenant; fortunately terra firma is resilient, and consequently our transgressions are not necessarily permanent. I wonder if the ancient Mayan civilization underwent a similar decay, defined by a progressive architectural abandonment? Their progeny could only gawk at the decomposed relics and wonder what had been lost. How had people lived and loved there?

A citizen of ancient Rome at its height could not fathom the empire's eventual demise. Now we only retain the language, architecture, and battlefield strategies, dreams that cannot come alive. The land of their exploits is scarred by chariot lanes, waterless aqueducts, and crumbling marble monuments. The planet is only a stage upon which human beings erect props as a backdrop to the act of their lives. Some spectacles have a long run and others fail miserably; howbeit, when the final curtain lowers, the theater reverts back to its barest brick walls and wooden floors. If only we could subsist within the parameters of Nature, instead pitting ourselves against it, perhaps the Earth would respond affirmatively.

Our route continues over a sturdy bridge, then through sucking muck, where my nose is overwhelmed with the intermingled aroma of chlorophyll, mud, and cedar. Within fifty yards we rise onto the surface of another abandoned road, along which three campsites are strung out on the deserted surface. Level, yes, but not picturesque, and though I hope Steve got here safe and sound two nights back, I'm delighted not to have to camp here.

The fern-lined track undulates gently through old-growth hemlock along the flanks of the North Puyallup River. As we traverse the hillside on a comfortably level course, the river can be heard tumbling farther and farther away down the mountain until it is only denoted by a homogeneous *swoosh*. A mile later the path arcs northwest for a more grueling climb up a tributary canyon.

Patrick advances ahead of me with a steady cadence, and, typical of most of the more arduous ascents, both of us retreat into our own inner thoughts and cajole our legs to complete the climb—of course I am too breathless to speak without stopping anyway. Heat, sweat, thirst, soreness, and slight fatigue, combined with the steady rhythm of stepping and the rocking of the pack on my shoulders, induces a trance of heightened sensations. The breeze whirling through the treetops, the rays of sunshine illuminating patches of lime green moss clinging to the tree trunks, the bear grass and huckleberry shrubs that crowd out the ferns for precious soil, and the red alder outlining the small stream to my left are all dreamlike visions.

By now the genuine personality of the Wonderland Trail has become manifest. It is rarely a gentle stroll, but prefers a leg-pounding downslope or muscle-burning upslope that tests every hiker. The extremes of elevation change usher us through a diversity of ecosystems, vacillating from one to another within minutes. While ascending away from the deep valley floor, the Douglas fir and hemlock have yielded to cedar and silver fir, which in turn are relinquishing the turf to subalpine fir and spruce, and ultimately they will concede to the tundra higher up.

After another mile, I catch up with Patrick, who is waiting in a patch of sunshine by the second of two elevated wooden bridges. The initial span extends over a dry gully, but the second fords a clear, cold, eight-foot-wide brook—an idyllic haven at which to reenergize my muscles with beef jerky and power bars, made palatable by fresh huckleberries.

This is the first day that we have tramped through the wilderness alone, on our own terms, for we have not encountered another human being for more than twenty-four hours. The solitude encourages consideration for those ephemeral thoughts I neglect to expound on at home. Only here, in the serenity of the wilderness, can I feel free to resolve my inner turmoil.

I am spellbound by a sunbeam illuminating a crystalline pool of water. The liquid cascades about slippery, gray boulders, to repose in this basin before plunging over a twenty-foot cliff, then tumbling down the hill-side to the North Puyallup River and flowing inevitably to the far-distant Pacific Ocean.

Multihued alder and maple leaves ply this waterway. Some commute on the surface, skimming by without pause in their haste to get off the mountain. Others hesitate, as if to appraise the ambiance of the locale, swirling about in a dance with kin. Sporadically a leaf settles down to the streambed to entwine with compatriots for a lengthy partnership, or perhaps even to compost collectively, their protoplasm requited to Nature to become fodder for another generation of life in this neighborhood. Water whirls in the eddies.

And what of the dilemma: to live carefree and brashly, or cautious and concisely? The former style implies exhilaration and satisfaction—to leave no stone unturned, story untold, or impulse unrealized. The casual contemplation of such an actuality elicits a feeling of exultant triumph. Notwithstanding, can that road truly be shared, or would it induce frustration and an abbreviated existence? Conceivably it would be preferable to be cautious, calculating, and secure, and thereby the fruits of senescence may be feasted upon. But will the amassed vigor match that of the impetuous proponent? All of us possess some measure of both characteristics, but have a modus operandi.

The movie *A River Runs Through It* is an agonizing yarn for me. Which brother should one feel sorry for in that story? Instinctually I lament the demise of Paul, the flamboyant, cheerful, younger brother. His penchant for the dramatic, extreme, and impulsive produces a colorful, unique, and memorable character, intoxicated with reality, perpetually present. This is in contrast to his older brother Norman, who is morose, hesitant, and cal-culating yet sensitive. That which Norman ultimately produces is refined, if not exceptional. But what has he forfeited?

Paul will not lose the exuberance of youth, but alas, he will not garner the truth of maturity. He will not discern the union of the Earth to its souls. He will not watch his garden mature, or its fruits ripen; he will not pluck and taste their succulence. What proof of his existence will endure? Someone's fond memory? How regrettable for the seasons to unfold without him, and the generations to reproduce without his ideological and biologic input.

Norman will experience a full life: son, brother, father, grandfather, husband, and lover. He will plant trees of humanity, tend them diligently, and watch them mature. He will pluck a bounty of love and savor the juices, but how bittersweet the taste. The aromas reminisce about entities lost—opportunities, people, and joy. Is the harvest of maturity refreshing when shared with ghosts? A bin of rancid savings. Has a calculated life led to an empty plate, when those who were bolder already had their fill and departed? Weathered footprints.

And what of yin and yang, the attraction of positive and negative, one plus one being greater than two? Is life enhanced by such arrangements, or is this the equation for mediocrity? The reckless energy of Paul is a prescription of adrenaline, stimulating the relatively inert Norman into actions he would not independently fathom. The calming effect of Norman allows Paul a paced vitality, so that his batteries can be recharged between surges of activity. Instead of bold black and pure white, perhaps this is the necessary gray of human existence. But are our souls here in this life to learn tolerance, coercion, moderation, and control, or should we throw loose the chains of codependence and take pleasure in life as an exuberant burst?

If two souls have differing courses and they happen to converge on the same highway, should they meld into the traffic, or instead diverge into a three-dimensional free-for-all with their pathways coexisting only for a moment? One may unwittingly follow others and gain from their knowledge, but then diverge effortlessly at the appropriate time. I fear this is a paradigm for loneliness, and a soul's potential unrealized. The leaves swirling in the stream do not question their fate, but they float blindly in the current without struggling and come to rest where they are meant.

Patrick putting on his pack snaps me out of my reverie. It is difficult to say what constitutes the ideal partner for an extended hike. More than a few parties have disintegrated in anger. Certainly similar physical abilities, dietary preferences, and hygienic practices are determinants; however, more important are the aesthetic goals: stop and smell the flowers versus sporting contest, for example. So far, Patrick and I have enhanced the trip for each other, giving space to freely explore, yet sharing interesting discoveries and thoughts. We are both patient and restless at the same time. We are not black-and-white characters mixing to a medium gray, but we have complemented each other.

Huckleberries

By the time I sort out my thoughts, we have ascended another half mile, exited the forest, and entered a landscape of huckleberry bushes and scorched trees. Hiking is a dance of three steps forward, pluck a handful of large, juicy huckleberries, savor their texture and taste in my mouth, and then saunter a few paces more, so that by the time we complete the final mile to the ridgetop, we are sated and relaxed.

The aftermath of a large forest fire in 1930 is still very evident here. What was once old-growth is now a ghost forest of silver snags, some with persistent black scars. Fallen comrades litter the ground, unconcealed by the dull green clumps of bear grass, whose tattered flower stalks are dismal remnants of the comely white torches of springtime. Cascade blueberry bushes grow prostrate among the weathered wood; unlike the red huckleberry bushes we previously encountered that were chest high, these barely get above our ankles. Their tones of red, gold, and brown, with plump blue berries decorating the foliage like large Christmas bulbs, are resplendent against the silvery wood. Their taste is not as tart and earthy as the huckleberries, but they are large, substantive, and very sweet, similar to ripe bananas, better than candy. I locate a log convenient to the abundant fruit and, firmly ensconced, blissfully gorge on the fruit.

Rolling a plump berry between my fingers, I reflect on the resemblance of their disguise to a Trojan Horse. The firm, yet pliable, skin protects both its flesh and seeds from the dehydrating sun and extreme weather. (The dark coloring no doubt maintains a comfortable temperature by absorbing the sun's rays.) The sugar-loaded body entices diners, so that a dose of seeds can be delivered. The seeds are the most amazing of all; already survivors of pollination and the challenges of growth, they must run a grueling gauntlet in order to successfully propagate. First are grinding teeth, threatening to shred and squash them into oblivion, then comes a caustic acid bath, followed by a prolonged transit through a slurry of digestive fluids, and only if they survive will they be released in a natural fertilizer. The hope is that they will be discharged at a prime growing location—not a good bet when humans are involved, so I'm sure they prefer to be consumed by a bear instead of by me.

The berries clearly exploit us and not vice versa. They could concoct a bitter flesh that no animal would touch, but in that case their seeds would drop only at the feet of the parent bush. Oh, how much more effective, but perilous, to seduce a stooge to transport them far and wide. I can imagine eons ago a tentative shrub bearing sweetened fruit to coax some beast to give them a ride, and subsequently, through the millennia, a mutually beneficial relationship developed between plant and animal. The bush generates a seed hardy enough to survive the rigors of the creature's digestive tract, and also wraps it in a nutritious packet that benefits the beast, which will reduce the bundle into a potent fertilizer to the benefit of the plant's progeny. As a side effect, or perhaps by intention, the richness of the fruit enhances the health of the living transport, who, with greater stamina, is capable of roaming more broadly, therefore expanding the home range of the ingenious plant. Of course a beast with a strong constitution will return through the years to consume more of the nutritious berries, and hence a partnership is forged. Just who is taking advantage of whom here?

Life on Rainier is intertwined into a tight weave. The trees do not exist independent of the soil. Though sometimes species are maliciously competitive, in the end they must all hold hands to survive. As John Daniel wrote in *Wilderness* magazine in response to a Reagan administration official's acerbic comment, "...he doesn't see the intricate webwork of fungi that strands through the ground, drawing its food from the roots of trees and helping the roots draw food from the soil. He doesn't see the red-backed vole that eats the fungi's fruiting bodies and disperses their spores, sheltering itself in downed rotting wood. He doesn't see the spotted owl that eats the red-backed vole, hunting in the dark through thousands of acres of trees...and feeding her owlets...as the Douglas firs keep growing and growing, each in turn going down, melting into the ground, sheltering the vole and feeding the fungi and holding the cold meltwater in its fragrant sponge."

Large or small, all life about Rainier is equally important. The *Homo* genus has always been an integrated member of the physical world, though we usually pretend that we're above it all. The thought of being devoured by a bear or ripped asunder by a shark rouses our ire (How dare they!), but once upon a time we may have been the favorite meal for some saber-toothed cat. However, most of the time humans have functioned at the top of the food chain, although we do not have the physical prowess of the other elite but instead employ the intellectual power of our brain to manipulate our surroundings and facilitate the capture of prey.

Before the arrival of Europeans, the Native Americans readily manipulated the environment. At Indian Henry's Hunting Ground they utilized an instrument of nature—fire—to promote rich grass growth; territory where valuable willow, alder, or fir thrived would have been finessed so that the desired species might flourish. They certainly did not raze the land to its basest dirt, and then convert it into whatever their whims desired, because—whether they knew about the interaction of truffles and trees is irrelevant—the integrity of the environment was respected. All organisms were perceived as important regardless of size or direct benefit to mankind. The early peoples of North America did not pretend to be gods.

Across the Puyallup Valley the boundary of Mount Rainier National Park ends and the clear-cuts begin, demarcated by brown, V-shaped, swaths of destruction; the "useless" shrubs, grasses, and trees are scraped into a slash pile and eliminated by burning. Unlike the Native American's ideology, the Forest Service does not foster the growth of indigenous flora, but instead inserts, into the ashes, the seedlings of the trees they most covet, a genetically homogeneous brood, which is selected for its lumber-producing qualities, but their similar susceptibilities to disease and weather extremes places them at risk for catastrophic obliteration. By comparison, the naturally occurring, heterogeneous forest is more resilient, more adaptable to the pressure of evolution. Western civilization's vain attempt at management is no more a forest than a cornfield is a prairie. Not only are we remiss to propagate such an offense, but we are arrogant to think we will get away with it. If we ever do succeed in tearing ourselves out of the fabric of life, we will be left naked, not in innocence, but exposed and alone.

Sunset Park is a fertile tapestry of coexistence sweeping uphill to the north then east, high above the forest from which we have just emerged. Boughless, sterling snags, underlain by a carpet of bear grass, reach up to the rocky cliffs of the Colonade; that precipitous ridge divides the glaciers that gravitate from the summit of Rainier itself. Chalky cumulus clouds romp among the ridge and mountaintops, composing fluffy puffs that obscure views, and feathery screens that resemble the handiwork of a watercolor artist.

To the northwest, the trail wanders through waves of knee-deep golden sedges, resembling a field of heather swaying in the wind, with subalpine firs splashed into the setting, creating an impressionistic painting. The beauty here hobbles my feet; ergo I shuffle forward half-heartedly. Reverently, we stroll northward under compact firs, around unpretentious, placid, dark pools, and through diminutive glades of lush green grass; all surfaces are coated with moist vegetation, with only the occasional bare gray rock rising free.

An abbreviated downgrade leads to the Golden Lakes Patrol Cabin, which indeed has a pond behind it, though the hue is more ebony than golden. The manmade structure bears resemblance to the cabin at Indian Henry's Hunting Ground, notwithstanding the less developed front porch. Trooping past the front door, we circle around the ridge that bounds the north shore of the lake. The lake is actually recessed in a bowl, with the seven designated campsites arranged on the northern brim, and a sheer one-hundred-foot cliff forming the northern wall; western bleeding heart grows among the pile of jagged rocks far below at the base of the bluff.

Dan at Golden Lakes Patrol Cabin

After consideration of their individual endearing qualities, we opt for campsite number four, which provides an optimal vantage point to look down upon two of the other Golden Lakes. Evidently these pools received their name based on distant visages, not a close encounter, considering they are also inky slates, encircled by a dense mysterious forest. What wild beasts prowl there? Adrenaline flushes my veins in anticipation of the emergence of some fearsome creature from out of the tangled cover, in search of fluid to quench its thirst. All is possible, as this is true wilderness—invigorating! Best of all, this perch will be our home for the next day and a half.

In the early evening, clouds drift in like a giant smokescreen restricting visibility, so that we decide to call it an early night and sprawl out in slumber. The following morning the lakes are still hidden by the dense fog, though the sun has arisen high above, providing light to this cool, gray day. After breakfast, Patrick and I wander off to our own pursuits.

I have elected to meander about the lakes and meadows, and, without the heavy backpack, it really does seem like a walk in the park. From the front porch of Golden Lakes Patrol Cabin, I survey the small wet meadow that is its front yard and the lanky red huckleberry brambles that form the border between field and forest; those previously savored, too-good-to-resist blueberries are mingled in the low-growing grasses. After a light snack, I continue along the path, past a knoll on which a small grove of firs roost beyond the reach of a shallow pond, until a six-inch-diameter clump of purplish bear scat captures my attention. On closer inspection the blob, principally huckleberries in various stages of digestion, is not steaming; accordingly it must have been deposited on some other day, though I do pray we get to see a bruin at some time during this trip.

The reminiscence about previous encounters with bears makes me chuckle, by virtue of the fact that my friends consider me a bear magnet and expect to see a bruin when they hike with me. I've spied two cubs peeking from around the trunk of an enormous California red fir they had climbed to escape from me, and my reciprocal curious glances at them were alternated with apprehensive scrutiny for their mother. Another time my dog, Mak, was chased by a bear, and the bruin pursued her back to within twenty feet of me. The hefty, muscular brute did not scamper away when he finally realized I was there, as would be typical of the majority of his kind, but instead postured threateningly for ten seconds or so, though it felt like hours. While he stood broadside, glaring over his shoulder, I perceived the steam of his hot breath and the drool at the corner of his mouth; he was fattening up for hibernation and clearly did not appreciate being disturbed. My legs wobbled for the next two miles to camp. On another occasion I was in the middle of a black bear triangle, each animal munching joyfully on spring's fresh grass, within a hundred yards of me. I am not tormented, but actually feel privileged to see such awesome creatures at close range, for they are a fantastic gift from Nature. Maybe we'll see one here.

The footpath drifts north, following the contour of the hillside, in order to stay above the soggy wetlands where shooting stars blossom in resplendent mauve rockets; then, beyond the distal shore of a lakelet, it reenters the old Sunset burn zone. A tiny spur trail on my right scrambles up into the heart of the scarred territory, but I am not in the mood for bushwhacking now. Rather, today is to be an amiable walkabout, like a peaceful Sunday picnic with friends and family. My companions are the hemlock, whose subtle incense I savor, the good-humored wild strawberries, and the cool, moist air. I lounge on my back in their midst, lolling about like a dog with legs to the heavens, then assume the perspective of a magenta paintbrush, vivaciously stretching into the air, hoping to seduce a mercurial hummingbird.

Bounding to my feet and up a hillock, I imbibe the energy of the surroundings. The Wonderland Trail descends northeast, narrowly evading an east-facing cliff, subsequently curving west under heavy forest cover, before reappearing as a faint horizontal scar crawling over an open saddle and plunging out of sight toward the Mowich River. Directly to the west, the two largest of the Golden Lakes intermittently disclose themselves two hundred feet below. The sun is dissipating the morning fog and producing a soft, diffused light that combats the burly, opaque clouds sailing up from the western valleys, crossing the lakes, filtering through the forest, and then percolating in and out of me.

Standing with feet firmly planted and arms spread wide, I close my eyes to sense the wind whirling through the treetops and ruffling my clothes. The sun every so often warms my cheeks; during its most penetrating moments my vision is filled with an inflamed burgundy, viewed from behind closed eyelids.

The lifeblood of the forest flows through me. Upon entrance into the wilderness my body was permeated with poison, now blown away by the vitalizing winds. The air downstream is momentarily polluted, but Nature is prodigious, capable, and willing to absorb my toxins. In its stead a restful elixir replenishes my soul; I breathe deeply, deliberately, and allow the cosmos to work its magic.

After some time—I have no idea how much—I drift back toward camp. Colors are more vibrant, birds sing more sonorously, and the breeze rocks me soothingly.

Patrick is seated on the front step of the patrol cabin, perusing the logbook. "Hey, you should read some of these passages. Some are really cool." Patrick has reviewed most of the entries in the half-inch-thick notepad; a thick, stubby pencil is the only instrument provided, thus those memos that were written by clammy hands are smeared. Patrick is leafing through the pages in order to point out some of his favorites: "I'm sitting here on the front porch with a bear feeding in the meadow not 50 feet from me." "Boots soaked. Pack soaked. Clothes soaked. It's been raining for four straight days since I left Longmire. I hear there's an awesome mountain out there somewhere. Having the time of my life!"

A light drizzle starts up and I'm envious for the relative comforts within this cottage. A gander through the glass panes reveals a wood stove primed for use, wool blankets warming a spartan bunk, and a kerosene lamp resting upon a small, rough-hewn wooden desk. A person sitting there scribbling a letter could pause from their task and peer out the window toward the southwest, beyond the woodpile, to the lake thirty feet yonder. Quite the enchanting lodge in which to while away the summer.

Stimulating by the domestic scene, Patrick asks if I am hungry. Neither of us has eaten anything substantial today, therefore my reply is unmitigated. "Yeah, definitely. But let's pick some of those sweet blueberries and I'll whip up some scones for dessert. There're some growing along the trail to camp." I had planned to pick them anyway, but four hands would definitely quicken the task.

Thankfully, he agrees with a "yummy." We return to our campsite after we have picked a cup or so of the sweet fruit. Once home, Patrick volunteers for the tedious and unenviable task of filtering water at the lake, while I get everything in order for supper. Fresh pond water for hot tea, and macaroni and cheese is boiled in the coffeepot; the fluid drained from the noodles adds body to hot chocolate. During the time that we chow down, the blueberry scone batter is cooking in the bakepacker, a convenient modification of a cooking pot that renders tasty fresh hot breads, cakes, etc. After the meal is polished off we enjoy a cup of hot spiced cider and relate our individual experiences of the day; following my report, Patrick especially wants to see the bear scat.

"So…what's it feel like to be out for more than four days? This is your first time; are you ready to pull out yet?" I jest with Patrick, when I know he has been enjoying himself, despite the physical challenges. The truth is that I am genuinely happy that he is so exhilarated by this extended escapade into the wilderness, as many people are hurting, bored, and ready to skedaddle by this time. Four days seems to be a dividing line, beyond which some folks decompensate and others excel.

There is no hesitation in Patrick's reply. "I love it. I can't believe how relaxed I feel." His voice resonates with affection and authenticity, and his demeanor is animated and passionate. "At first I just wandered about the lakeshore looking at tracks in the mud, then I went over to camp five. You know, the one over there at the edge of the cliff," he says, nodding his head and pointing over his shoulder to the west. The spot discussed has a wooden bench from which to admire the sunset, and, because it is on a corner of the ridge, it has an extensive view over the lakes and woods.

I am curious if he has witnessed any bear, elk, or other large mammal venturing from concealment. "Did you see anything down by the lakes?"

"No. Most of the time the lakes were lost in the clouds. In fact, I could hardly see below me at all. The cliff seemed to step off into nothing," he relates quietly, in the manner of recalling a distant whimsical dream.

I am intrigued, wanting to hear the details of this experience, which has obviously moved him. "So did you read or something?"

"A little, but most of the time I just meditated," he replies blandly, without providing any further details.

"Very cool. We hardly get a chance to do that at home," I tease him. This prompts him to explain in greater depth.

"The thing is, I found this level spot of ground right at the edge of the cliff. The fog totally engulfed me at times, although I could still feel and see the bright sun above, burning through, warming me. By that point my body seemed to let go and completely relax." Patrick is acting out the scene, pulling in the fog, sweeping away the clouds, and now drooping his shoulders in relaxation. "I was expecting my muscles to be tight and sore from the hike, but instead they felt strong and supple, as if all the negative energy in my body was replaced with positive. And it was not just a physical, but a spiritual warming too." He cups his mug of hot cider, while peering absently into the flame flickering from the stove.

"I am so excited that you like this as much as I do," I offer warmly, then add, after a reflective pause, "There is no way to explain this to someone who hasn't been here."

"I love it," he adds emphatically.

By now the hot cider has been drained, and we are surprised to realize that during our reveries the clouds have lifted and the sun has appeared low on the horizon. The trees reflect a warm, golden glow that transitions to a rosy hue; darkness chases the rich pastel color up the mountain, and behind us, Mount Rainier has emerged, presiding over day's end. The sun's gentle kiss softens the ridgelines, causing the mountain to blush; in that spell, steely blue surrenders to gray, though the glaciers high above never fully concede to the darkness.

Patrick and I are reluctant to retire to the tent, and instead heat up another pot of water for soothing hot chocolate. The sun-driven winds breathe their last gasp before surrendering to the stillness of the night. The forest is no longer scary and threatening, but has metamorphosed into a cherished friend. We both now feel surrounded by benevolent family, engulfed tenderly by the love of this wilderness.

Mowich Crossing

Now let me tell you about satori, a Zen concept. Satori is the warrior's state of being; it occurs at the moment when the mind is free of thought, pure awareness; the body is active, sensitive, relaxed; and the emotions are open and free…

DAN MILLMAN, *WAY OF THE PEACEFUL WARRIOR*

The unhurried day of soulful meditation was sublime, but I rouse from my slumber in a restless mood. Sunbeams radiate from the orb that is still hidden by the hulk of Rainier. Hot coffee is gulped down while dismantling camp, and then, with a nod of farewell to the ranger cabin, we are in motion again.

Our legs warm up during the initial two miles, a lenient saunter in and out of forest, through meadows, and past small lakes, arcing around the Golden Lakes Basin. Waist-high huckleberry bushes are a muted crimson, blushing under the influence of the crisp air, which hints of autumn. The west-draining valley plunges out of the park and into the clutches of the wood-products industry, where the unmistakable rumble of a timber truck is readily heard chugging along the dirt logging road in the midst of the clear-cut hillsides. Even here, the impact of man on this planet is palpable.

After a few miles we pause at an open saddle to decipher the map. Somewhere across those ravines and crags is the pathway to Mowich Lake. The trail curves northeast and drops from an elevation of 4,600 feet here, to 2,700 feet at the dangerous ford of the South Mowich River. "This is one rugged river, and there may or may not be a log crossing…there was a deep waterfall cascading over the log bridge in the afternoon. Early the next morning the water had dropped a foot and a half," the guidebook cautions. Besides the compulsion to move, this potential peril instigated our early departure.

I lead the brisk descent, propelled by a desire to remain high and dry, but within a mile I realize that Patrick has drifted farther and farther behind and has vanished in the woodland. Assuredly, the past few days have demonstrated that I am faster on the downhill and Patrick rules on the uphill, but not by this large of a margin. With apprehension for his welfare, I wait at the pivot point of a lengthy switchback for him to catch up.

I feel as if I have been flying along the sheer hillside through the old-growth hemlock and cedar, with their crowns at the level of my feet. In the forest clearing behind me, raspberry bushes and vine maples grow in the midst of moss-covered boulders, and a chickadee trills his happy song as he flits among the branches. The forest essence soothes me for a full ten minutes before I finally spot Patrick strolling down the trail. No limp. No blood. No sweat. Just what has he been doing?

"Are you okay? I can slow down if you need to," I ask with genuine concern, despite his unblemished appearance.

Patrick's face looks totally relaxed, and his gaze absently sweeps through me surveying the environs. "I'm fine. It's just this forest is so…I don't know…incredibly alive." He mumbles, looking totally dumbfounded, as if he is so internally perplexed that he cannot possibly explain his feelings to me. His eyes continue to rove, embarrassed by this exposure of his core.

"I know. I feel like I've been flying through the trees. You know…the trail is so steep that the treetops are at eye level one minute, midtrunk the next, and then, all of a sudden, I'm walking across their roots. It's a magical feeling." Patrick finally makes eye-to-eye contact with me, bearing a hopeful expression; maybe I can identify with his sentiment after all.

"Well there's that, but it's so much more," he utters with a quiet, yet decisive inflection. "It's hard to describe." Despite the light sweat and shoulders sagging under the weight of his backpack, Patrick looks totally at ease.

I am relieved that he is unharmed, but now I am curious as to why he is hiking so slowly. Isn't he as nervous about the river crossing as I am? "Did you see something?"

He is snapped out of his reverie by my goading him to clarify his innuendo. "No. No animals or anything. It's more what I feel."

"Like what?" Just spit it out!

"Well, this might sound stupid, but I've been stopping to feel the trunks of the trees," he explains a coyly. "They have such incredible energy." His eyes lock on mine, searching for anything but ridicule.

I wave of awareness washes through me. He is right; we should live in the present, the bridge be damned. My voice is one of reassurance: "That's cool. I often run my hands over the bark of different trees to feel their various textures."

Emancipated from his insecurities, Patrick is more animated, with a fascinated look on his face. "Well that too, but there was this humungous tree back there that I just had to lay my hands on. You know, palms lightly on the trunk, not rubbing it—it felt like the tree was touching back"

"So was it pushing you away?" I encourage him.

"No, it was kinda like…I could feel this low humming energy," his voice rises in a slow crescendo. "It was so positive, and kinda enveloped me. My whole being became calm and relaxed."

"Very cool," I murmur while he continues.

"Yeah, and I kept thinking, 'This great old tree has a story to tell.' You know…about his neighbors, and the forest life around him." Patrick acts out the scenario of his hands massaging the hemlock, his neck extending to behold the forest canopy.

"I bet," I agree empathetically.

Patrick carries on with his re-creation, as if in a trance. "After that I had the urge to touch all the trees along the way, especially the bigger ones. I just couldn't resist; each tree made me more relaxed—more a part of the surroundings."

"No longer a foreigner passing through," I interject softly.

"Exactly! It's like I can't be separated from anything here; I'm part of the whole. I took a deep breath every time I touched a tree, trying to swallow it in. I wanted to feel this connection, I sought it out," he concludes emphatically.

"That's cool." I applaud him. "You're absolutely right; that's exactly why we should be taking our time."

We resume our hike at a more moderate pace in order to soak in the vitality of the forest. The poisons of our everyday existence had been purged and now the lifeblood of creation is rushing in, like osmosis; it is not in my power to halt it, nor do I want to. I am kindred to the cedar and the sparrow, equally. It would not startle me if the birds should converse and the trees walk about—transported back to a time when all breathing and non-breathing entities were family.

The rumble of the South Mowich River becomes steadily more vociferous as we near the wide, gravel streambed. The slope eases onto the floodplain, where we cross paths with a sociable, forties-something couple, who are headed to Golden Lakes. "I thought we would be seeing you about now," the cheerful woman enthusiastically greets us.

I stammer dumbfounded. "Excuse me?" Most unforeseen interactions are comprised of a nod, "hello," or cursory dialogue pertaining to the weather or trail conditions, but she behaves as if she knows us.

"I was just saying to my husband that if anyone stayed the night at Golden Lakes, they should be getting to the crossing pretty soon," she clarifies with an "I told you so, honey" tone to her voice.

"Ooohhh." Now it makes sense. I can disregard my knee-jerk paranoia and profit from this excellent opportunity for a scouting report. "How is the river?"

"Well there is a little water splashing on the log, but it's not too bad," she replies deferentially. The fact that they made it across allays some of my fears, but she implies that we better not dawdle.

"Thanks. Have a great hike." My good-bye is a bit abrupt, but I can almost feel the humid swelter of the midmorning rapidly melting the glacier upstream, unleashing a rising flood of murky frothing liquid to surge downstream and engulf the bridge. My stride becomes progressively more swift and urgent—no time to waste.

Though the track is level it is difficult to sprint the remaining half mile to the river through this intriguing, lush rainforest. The area greatly resembles the Hoh Rainforest in Olympic National Park, where Patrick and I had endured four chilly wet days last March; the memory invokes an involuntary shiver, but also a smile. Green is definitely in vogue, with the immense spruce trees sporting a coat of Irish moss, the incongruously gigantic blades of the big leaf maples dangling listlessly in the still air, and the huge fronds of devil's club acting as warning flags to stay clear of their piercing thorns. Each free drop of water emigrates into the multitude of narrow, but deep, streams wending their way underneath, around, and occasionally spilling over the roots of the behemoths. Our pathway is made clear by a multitude of sturdy wooden bridges; otherwise these channels would be cursed instead of romanticized. Suddenly the forest parts and we emerge into the dazzling sunlight bathing the riverway.

Spring snowmelt and glacial surges have rasped the South Mowich River's bed into a wide rocky byway, purged of all vegetation except for a few brave flowers. The stream itself is discordantly small as it gushes along the edge of the forest near the opposite bank. We pick our way across the gravel and stones, which are smooth and weathered from bouncing along in the torrent, until the raging water, creamy with silt as it drags a part of the mountain along with it to the sea, is nigh. There is no way to determine its depth, for even in the eddies one can only see a few inches down; therefore, if a calm stretch existed, which it doesn't, the crossing would be exceedingly dangerous without a bridge—although the log spanning the torrent is hardly substantial.

Patrick and I stare with dismay at the narrow beam that is anchored in the gravel at either side of this raging current. Only six inches wide, its tread has been chopped out of the spindly timber to shape a torqued, rough, slanted tread, and to intensify our internal gut wrenching, there is now water lapping onto the far end of the plank. Surely there must be another way across, I think to myself, but a hasty survey confirms that this is it.

Well if I am nervous, I'm sure Patrick is doubly so, hence I brace myself to appear confident for his sake. I am certain that he has never crossed anything like this before, especially with a pack on his back. After a pep talk, I move downstream to a position where the river rounds a bend and I might be able to catch him if he gets swept away, and then signal him to start across. Step by step Patrick eases across. Fortunately the thundering rapids are so loud that it covers up the sound of our knees knocking. I dare not request him to stop and wave to the camera, though it would be an outstanding shot. At moments he hesitates with trepidation, but the last few strides are more certain, and he dismounts the bridge sporting a broad, relieved grin. My turn!

Dan crossing the South Mowich River

Using the ice ax as a balancing pole, I start the heel-to-toe traverse. It is not so much the slenderness, irregularity, or even the slipperiness of the expanse that evokes fear and doubt. (If this tree trunk were stationed in a playground, children would be running across it.) No, the most unnerving factor is the continuous motion of the water rushing swiftly from right to left beneath the log. The vast majority of my field of vision is permeated with a vertigo-inducing froth of speeding liquid. My consciousness is totally focused on the unmoving timber, which appears to float in space, while nullifying the swirling water underneath. This is truly living in the present—no time to be distracted, even for consideration of the consequences of falling. My sole awareness is the position of my right leg, the pressure of my weight shifting to my left foot, and the response of the wood to my contact. Seldom in my life am I this awake.

The fording of South Mowich River took only a few seconds, but it will be indelibly printed in my mind. Once on the other side I realize that, in our apprehension, neither of us had remembered to unfasten our pack belts; good thing we didn't dive in, as the packs would have dragged us under to a watery grave.

I sigh fully and look over at Patrick, who is beaming happily. "I'm so proud of myself. I always thought I was too chicken to do something like that. I can't believe I did it," he declares haltingly, but exultantly.

"Yeah, you made it. South Tahoma Bridge and now this. There are no obstacles anymore," I tease him.

"This whole trip is something I never thought I would do. It's all such a sweet victory." On that note he turns and strides confidently off of the gravel bar and into the woods.

Among the streamside alder and hemlock is the South Mowich Shelter and campsites, which are surprisingly close to the river, and I am sure raging springtime meltwater periodically deluges them. After a full, adventurous morning we welcome the chance to take a breather in this placid setting. Leaning our packs against the open front quarter of the building, we cast aside our boots and socks to dry, and then clamber around the worn wooden floor of the square log structure that is enclosed on three sides. Protein bars and strawberry-yogurt-covered pretzels are nibbled while reviewing the map. This feels like a lunchtime recess—an intermission between the rushed morning descent, intent on crossing the river, and the afternoon ascent to Mowich Lake.

With the brief respite concluded, we stroll across North Mowich River on an elevated and much more massive log, complete with handrail. From here the trail rises twenty-six hundred feet in the three and a half miles to Mowich Lake, and then it is another mile and a half to Eagle's Roost. Climb, climb, climb. The passage is somewhat monotonous in the heavily forested hillside, with very limited views. I gauge our progress by the proximity of Hessong Rock, which pokes out of the forest in the east like a lone sentinel; our route from Mowich Lake to Eagle's Roost skirts along its base. Difficult as the hiking is now, it cannot compare to what Dr. William Tolmie must have encountered in 1833.

A twenty-one-year-old recent graduate of Glasgow Medical School, he had sought out the wilderness. Getting permission from the chief trader at Fort Nisqually on the mouth of that namesake river, he had traveled for ten days from Puget Sound to this area, under the guise of collecting medicinal herbs. Five Nisqually guides, including La-ha-let, accompanied him on his "botanizing expedition" up the Puyallup River then overland to the Mowich River drainage. Somewhere in my present vicinity they decided to proceed up the north branch of the Mowich River, undoubtedly with their eyes fixed upon prominent Hessong Rock that was standing proud over its forested realm. I can imagine him slogging along this slope, pausing to examine calypso orchids, yerba buena, yellow wood violets, vanilla leaf, and deer fern; ultimately he may have culminated on the ridge high above Spray Park, between Hessong Rock and Mount Pleasant, but no one knows with certainty. I envision him halting on a bare crest of rock and whirling around to soak in the magnificence of Mount Rainier; perhaps he knew then that he was the first European to stand on its broad shoulders.

The steady upward march is a test of physical and mental endurance; hereinafter I try to occupy my mind by observing every rock, tree, stone, and flower, looking for something unique to explain the mysteries of the universe. In the heat of the afternoon that dreamy feeling overwhelms me again. My attention is drawn to the workings of my body, as if I am watching it labor from the outside: muscles hot and straining to lift my mass skyward, rapid and rhythmical beating of my heart, and the cadence of my respiration. Left foot forward breath in, right foot forward breath out; any rate faster than that and I would succumb to fatigue.

Patrick interrupts my trance to discuss our plans; he is contemplating just getting to Mowich Lake and pitching the tent there for the night. That strategy sounds pretty good right now, especially when I remember the youngster with the family of five saying something about a shower being there. A smile creeps onto my face; now that is motivation! Finally the sound, and then sight, of the cascading waters of Crater Creek falling from Mowich Lake above announce that our ascent is ending.

Once on the far side of the stream we ignore the sign pointing to Eagle's Roost, and instead veer northward up the steep, slippery quarter mile to the lake, where we have resolved to spend the night if it is even half decent.

The sweet satisfaction in attaining our target for the day, Mowich (Chinook for deer), is tempered by the less than rustic appearance of the locale. Does and fawns no longer glide through an ephemeral primeval forest, but are forced to dart across the packed dirt road engineered by Bailey Willis. Signs direct us to the tent sites, which, unfortunately, are plopped down on the hardpan of an abandoned parking lot, denuded of all trees, and in plain view of the twenty or so cars lined up nearby; their occupants wandering here and there. The sole appeal to the campground are the lake and the picnic tables. Fatigued and sore, we stow our backpacks on one of them, and evaluate the campsites.

My first impression of this scenario is repugnance, but I am tired, and accordingly focus on more basic needs. The recollection that there might be showers here momentarily brightens my outlook; they would definitely salvage the situation. Aaaahhh! I drink about a liter of water, and feast on peanut yogurt Ironman bars and chunks of Hershey's chocolate, before wandering over to the most likely candidate to house a shower. Ironically, the concrete block structure contains the foulest smelling pit toilets in which I have ever been. Holding my nose, literally, I remain in the putrid building only long enough to ascertain that there are no showers. Somewhat dejected, I rendezvous with Patrick beside the packs, and we empty our trash (lighten our loads!), then drift over near the ranger's cabin along the lakeshore, in order to debate our next course of action.

We are equally exhausted, but Patrick is more willing to stay here than am I. It is true that this sizable lake has its enticements; fifty feet away from us right now is a mother teaching her two preschool-age children how to catch fish from the deep blue waters. A congenial, elderly park ranger is moving rocks about in a wheelbarrow and casting them strategically to hinder the encroachment of gallivanting tourists upon the grassy meadows alongside the meandering exit stream. He nods a friendly greeting, which we return from our position on the shoreline.

"I know you're tired, but it's only a mile and a half to Eagle's Roost, and it's essentially level," I coax Patrick, because I really don't want to remain here tonight.

Patrick twists his body to his left to scan the campground and shrugs his shoulders slightly. "This isn't so bad...considering how I'm feeling," he replies indifferently.

His irresolute inflection infers a lack of conviction, so I might have a chance to convince him to continue on to Eagle's Roost. "Come on... we can make it," I implore. Indeed, after further rest, food, water, and another glance at the mediocre setting, Patrick agrees to move on; albeit with second thoughts about having prevailed upon him, I have faith in his determination and willpower. Best of all, once committed to the task, he proceeds full bore without complaint, traits I sincerely admire and appreciate, as they also make us a good hiking partnership, compensating for my single-mindedness. (I tend to push some companions beyond their comfort level, and not know when to stop.) Furthermore, Patrick is as desirous as I am to be rewarded for this hard day's hike with an emotionally becalming campsite. Consensus achieved, the packs are swiftly reloaded. "Let's get it over with," Patrick urges as he buckles his waist belt, and then takes the lead, retracing our steps back down the trail.

The pathway rambles on gradual slopes around Hessong Rock, though one stretch, resembling an abrupt miniature staircase, near Eagle Cliff Overlook tests my reserve. By the time I get to the top of it, I have no energy to spare for the one-hundred-foot side trip to the viewpoint, which the guidebook reports is a stunning view of everything west, appreciated from the edge of a rock jutting out from the cliff into space. Despite the retaining fence, I'm not certain that my quivery legs will hold steady and prevent me from pitching over the edge, so I stumble onward, past the day-trippers beating a retreat to their cars. In another half mile we arrive at the junction with the side trail to camp, where the tent sites are scattered amid the trees to my right, fifty feet lower than the main trail.

Eagle's Roost Camp is a nest snuggled upon the cliff. To the west the earth plummets away into thin air; to the east and north the sheer flanks of Hessong Rock form an insurmountable backstop; to the south a large stream pours by tantalizingly close, yet unreachable, except by a tremendous expenditure of effort. The site itself isn't perfectly flat but is a rounded mound, with the seven tent platforms perched on the few relatively level spots available. There is only one other group of overnighters here, and they are hardly visible over the rise from our location. After nimbly assembling camp, we gather supplies to filter water, scrub clothes, and cleanse our bodies, and then saunter up the trail toward Spray Park.

Within a quarter mile we hurdle two clear, gurgling brooks via rustic wooden bridges and then detour via a side trail to the base of Spray Falls. It is a spectacular sight, cascading four hundred feet off a rocky plateau. As the water plunges it widens into a frothy ribbon before diving into a deep pool, with the early evening sun creating rainbows in the mist. Shouting over the booming reverberation of the falls, we concur that this is a superb way to wash away the sweat and toil of a challenging day. With dusk imminent, we are confident that no one will happen by to witness our revels in the whitewater, therefore we strip out of our clothes and splash in the chilly water. The massaging current invigorates my muscles; the inflammation is mollified. Oh what a grand and full day!

Spray Falls

I breathe fully the misty air, water dripping from my hair. Lanky blue-bells hug the banks in the company of pink and yellow monkey-flowers, crimson columbine, vetch, and currants. After our apparel is rinsed and laid out on the rocks to dry, we both sprawl on the streamside and bask in the illuminating evening sunshine that is softening into the western horizon. I feel like aboriginal man. Absolutely grand!

Suddenly we spring into motion, triggered by the materialization of a solitary hiker, whose stealthy approach was covered by the roaring torrent. He seems somewhat miffed by the display of our gear strewn hither, and curtly rock-hops across the stream, snaps a few pictures of the waterfall, and departs posthaste, leaving us in privacy with Spray Falls once again. Yet the primordial aura has been dispelled, so we gather our things and retreat to camp.

The brisk bath has reenergized my being. I mentally skip along the path, absorbed by the waning beams of twilight that waft through the hemlocks and faintly highlight the soft green moss clinging to the slate gray bark; a slight breeze stirs the branches and lichen. To my surprise, my body is not exhausted, but is gratified by such a bounteous day. My mind is fulfilled, not wearied. Only my stomach pleads for satisfaction.

Following such a calorie-burning day, I'm hungry for anything with a high fat content; macaroni and cheese, and pasta with seasoned mayonnaise sound yummy. Thank the person who invented foil pouches! The WhisperLite stove is fired up, and the meal consumed immediately after it is drained from the boiling water; then ginseng tea soothes my palate. This is such a peaceful site.

The sun glimmers faintly as it disappears behind the westward-flowing Mowich River and over the distant Pacific Ocean. At Mowich Lake the trail had veered east as it rounded the first bend in our circuit. The west leg of our quest is concluded, and we now begin the traverse across the northern shoulder of Rainier.

The guidebook describes the coming stretch as a series of far-reaching sub-alpine meadows sweeping up the mountain, with the pathway running through their heart, indulging voyagers with expansive vistas of all northern Washington. Tomorrow will assuredly be one of the highlights of our entire trek. With a cup of hot chocolate, we toast our decision to tackle the final two miles to this beautiful campsite; moreover, we cheer the fact that we are now positioned to enter extraordinary Spray Park early tomorrow morning. In the darkness my eyes close in blissful slumber—a fitting reward for such a splendid day.

We are getting around this mountain after all!

Storm Clouds In The Darkness

The Chickadee lives by joyous faith in living. Whenever everything else curls up and prepares to wait, or die, the chickadee is out in the middle of it. I have heard them even in the middle of a blizzard, chirping with that dancing tone over and over into the cold air, as if it thinks that hiding from a storm is the craziest form of self-denial.

TOM BROWN, JR., *THE TRACKER*

Dawn arose expectantly on the seventh day of our adventure. Today we would reap the dividends of yesterday's challenges. Visions of flowers, meadows, and majestic peaks permeate my thoughts as I wipe the sand from my eyes, but, unfortunately, when I throw open the tent flap, I am greeted by an opaque bank of cool fog.

Last night's sublime sunset had falsely forecast that today would be a marvelous display of blue skies and dazzling sunshine; however, the mountain whimsically composes its own clime. Nevertheless, I am optimistic that the clouds will burn off with the morning's warmth, and expectantly I flop back down and snooze for another hour before brewing coffee, playing cards, partaking of breakfast, making a second pot of coffee, and waiting—ever more impatiently. By noon the visibility is actually further reduced by a cold white mist rising with increasing density from the enshrouded valley below, imparting the appearance that the camp is balanced on the edge of a vast abyss. Rainier has chosen to be obscure today.

Our packs are lighter, our legs stronger, and we are anxious to see what lies ahead of us, so we tarry no longer; being mad is pointless. Anyway, inclement weather can facilitate memorable outings, when your vitality and vulnerability are readily palpable; therefore we proceed with a sense of adventure.

After refilling our bottles in the first icy stream, we switchback up the ridge between two cascades that plummet down from the high meadows. Within a half mile the trail levels off, then crosses Grant Creek—lined with Lewis monkey-flower, scouter's corydalis, and larkspur—and soon bursts into Spray Park proper. By now the mist has condensed into light rain and the wind whips about more insistently, blowing the damp air through any loose seam in my clothing to bathe me in a clammy sweat and prompting us to halt and rummage through our packs for fleece tops and Gore-Tex rain jackets, which we don for the first time on this journey. (I usually disdain rain pants unless it is absolutely necessary.) I also stash the camera in the driest nook of my pack that I can find. Lastly, the backpack itself is enveloped with its own waterproof cover.

During our scrambles an obstinate gray jay has flown in to doggedly beg us for a meal from his post atop a six-foot-tall subalpine fir. I'm sure with his degree of persistence that he eats well here. His cry floats across the meadow, rising into the misty fog and careening through the low-growing azure lupine, cardinal Indian paintbrush, and chalky-hued heather, which embellish the ankle-high sedges. Scattered clusters of firs emerge fleetingly from the haze, like dark specters. As we prepare to recommence, a small troop of day-hiking senior citizens stomps past us into the meadow; we delay a few moments to give them space, before continuing uphill along the cattle path.

The trail keeps to the meadow, with only brief respites from the cold, moisture-laden wind under the cover of the trees. Huddled within the groves are multiple cliques of day-trippers—most appear to be retired folk—snacking on crackers, cheese, and apples. On some other bright day we would be oohing and ahhing about the flowers, ridges, valleys, and possibly even bears surrounding us. Indeed, the violet bog gentian, rosy spirea, pink wandering daisies, and leatherleaf saxifrage are splendid, even in this murk. However, my attention is drawn ever more insistently to the cool dampness of my legs, the sound of Gore-Tex rubbing across my ears, and the feel of pumice gravel grinding under my feet.

A mile or so into the meadow we are met by a husband and wife descending from above. They both appear to be in their early sixties, in good shape, and, despite the relentless drizzle, they both are upbeat, with perky smiles upon their faces. The woman retracts the visor of her Gore-Tex coat slightly so that she can readily examine our faces, but not so far as to permit the stinging pellets of wind-driven rain to strike bare flesh. The gentleman is well over six feet tall, and, because he is standing uphill from Patrick and me, he stoops a bit to greet us, while twisting his head to keep dry.

"So where are you guys headed?" he asks with a firm intonation, to ensure he is heard over the cacophony of the gales.

Patrick leans forward and shouts his reply. "We're doing the Wonderland Trail!"

The fellow nods his head affirmatively and tightens his chin as if in contemplation of, and simultaneously impressed with, our undertaking. "You just get started?"

"No, we've been out seven days now. Started at Longmire," Patrick rejoins choppily. "How about you guys?"

The woman is rubbing her gloved hands together in front of her chest; still sporting her affable expression, she tips her head to her right to defer the answer to her husband, who, without hesitation, outlines the circumstances of their excursion. "We climbed up to the ridge, at the top of Spray Park. Unfortunately the weather kept getting worse instead of clearing off as we had hoped. No view whatsoever." He peers up into the heavy mist and shakes his head negatively for a second, and then concludes emphatically, "So we're heading back to Mowich Lake."

"Too bad," I pipe in. "It doesn't seem like it's going to clear off." We all pivot an instant, in hope of detecting a breach in the gloom, but to no avail.

The quiet pause in conversation is broken as the chap brightens up with a flash of insight. "You guys probably haven't heard a forecast in a while. I heard the prediction for the next few days, if you're interested." It's apparent from his demeanor that he is zealous to impart this intelligence and only seeks permission as a reflexive courtesy, but to his consternation I dissent.

"That's okay," I decline casually with a shrug of my shoulders.

His mouth freezes in contortion as he expectantly has to bite his tongue, and then he stammers to clarify my response. "You don't want to know what it's supposed to do over the next few days?" he retorts, obviously disbelieving that I actually heard him.

"No, really, it wouldn't make any difference anyway," I reassure him with a good-natured smirk.

I imagine, by the way he shifts from left to right, that he thinks I am crazy to not crave this vital information. He resolutely leans forward to be certain he has comprehended me unmistakably. "Seriously, you don't want to know?" he demands loudly and clearly, while scanning my face for an inkling of rationality. I sense his need to enunciate his scoop, but I don't want the burden.

"Yeah, seriously, I really don't want to know," I confirm evenly. I nod positively, then glance at Patrick and note that he is in agreement, at which point I chuckle and readdress the couple. "I hope you guys have a good hike out." With that Patrick and I scoot past them and launch ourselves up the trail into the clouds. Over my shoulder I sneak at look at the woman tugging on her husband's coat sleeve to start him down the trail; he has such an incredulous expression.

My behavior might strike one as being rude or stupid, but the information the fellow was so eager to relay would have imposed a counterproductive distraction: expectation. I had dreamed of the radiant sunset mirrored by Golden Lakes, but it evaded me; still, Klapatche Park was divine. If I hadn't read the guidebook describing the splendors of Spray Park, I would be quite content and enchanted with that which currently flourishes within a stone's throw of me. How would being familiar with a meteorologist's prediction add to my blissful station: skepticism in its relevance, or surprise with its accuracy? If tomorrow was guaranteed to be sunny we could circle back to Eagle's Roost and wait, or if rain was expected for the next two days we could hunker down in some protected locale and beseech the sun to please hurry back. Yet, momentum impels me forward; I will witness Rainier as it reveals itself and not be aggravated by predictions. The chap scurrying down the trail will have to shoulder the disappointment.

Such contemplation keeps me company in my cocoon of waterproof fibers. My mind is liberated by wildness. My innate senses are free to analyze the animal prints, the scent of the trees, the force of the wind on my bare skin, and the intrigue of randomly encountered strangers. The hypnotizing cadence of my gait assists in centering me, for fleeting instants, in the present; past and future are suspended. Backpacking is meant to be a series of unpredictable events that test your patience, gauge your resilience, and tickle your fancy.

For the past half hour Patrick and I have been alone on the nebulous flanks of the mountain. The trail has been rising steadily toward the crest over which lies Seattle Park. With the temperature relentlessly dropping, I am wrapped in thick dew on the verge of being a chilling frost. The wind is howling with increasing vigor.

The fine pumice crunches underfoot with an oddly pleasurable sensation, interrupted by occasional bounds up firm lava outcrops. Ever-shrinking subalpine firs cower in the mist, their trunks boldly shouldering the gales and their boughs thrown alee, affording an ephemeral shelter during the few paces on their cushioning needles. Sedges rarely venture here, instead preferring the loamy streamside soils; however, a few flowers flourish, hugging the coarse gravel in order to lessen the bite of the harsh weather. Dwarf lupines, which are identical to those giants previously viewed, can now fit in the palm of my hand; bell heather form green masses sprinkled with white petals; paintbrush, cinquefoil, shooting stars, lousewort, and pussytoes, all splashed with dew, abound in miniature.

It is fascinating how the plants pull water into themselves. For example, creamy white winds are swirling around the evergreen boughs, which knock the life-giving moisture out of the air and drop it to their mouths under my feet; the muted whistle produced is a pleasing side effect.

The trees fade into mere shrubs as we abandon all protection to traverse progressively larger snowfields, with the heavens shrieking to drown out all conversation. In the disorienting murk, we point out to each other the old, dirty footsteps etched in the crusty white snow and the occasional orange-splashed rocks that denote our path. I swear that native spirits are accosting us with a screeching reproach; if I can just flip back the rain hood quick enough, I will see a shaman keening on the ridge crest. A spine-tingling, high-pitched wail of lament for a fallen warrior, buried in the boulders nearby. Ceaselessly repeating his piercing cry.

A few hesitant steps onward bring reality to my hallucinations. Jet-black ravens caw and render a muffled *whoosh* as they flap their glistening wings a few times to catch the current, gliding through the dwarf trees and shooting off the cliff. We have arrived at the apex from which we will descend into Cataract Valley and our camp for the night.

As we begin to drop, the clouds opt not to follow and we can see lush, emerald meadows a thousand feet down. Astoundingly, life abounds even here. Fat ground squirrels shrill their warning and dash for cover in a pile of lava rocks; avalanche lilies decorate the ground recently vacated by snow.

The ensuing quarter mile is a combination of sliding and boot skiing down a snowfield to a bare earth gap, where we drink from a pure snowmelt trickle. While partaking of the icy refreshment, we are greeted by the first person we have encountered since the "weatherman." This character is no fair-weather, preppy, city dweller, but instead is a dirty, forty-ish man with weathered skin, gruff beard, and rotting teeth. It is soon apparent that he is also gregarious and talkative. While leaning forward on an inch-thick hiking staff, he explains in a staccato voice that today he is doing the fifteen-mile loop up Carbon River Valley, then returning via Mowich Lake.

When we tell of our progress around the mountain he lightens up in kinship, by virtue of our status as "loop" hikers. I can relate to his communion. In hiking the Pacific Crest Trail across Oregon I felt a certain pity for, and reserve toward, day-trippers, but upon meeting fellow "through" hikers I would immediately connect with them. We would exchange notes on our experiences, where we were going, and how our lives allowed us the time required to walk that trail.

Currently, it is evident that this disheveled hombre is going through a similar bonding process with us. After all, who can really understand what it is like to be out in the wilderness, hefting on your back all the materials you will need for the next two weeks? He is as restless as us and soon heads off, subsequent to a parting recommendation to stop at Longmire and purchase a tall walking stick like his, adorned with the Wonderland Trail emblem to verify to all that we had completed our journey; somewhat like joining an exclusive club.

Shortly we stomp over the last snow patch and take a break on a promenade overlooking several valleys that descend like fingers toward the wide wrist of the Carbon River far below. Once the insulation of our packs is stripped off, we are both downright cold, and again forage in the rucksacks to procure fleece pants, rain pants, wool gloves, and a hat to retain our heat, and beef jerky to fuel our body furnaces. Water dipped from a three-foot-wide stream rehydrates us.

Patrick in Seattle Park above the distant Carbon River

Clearly visible underneath the roof of thick cumulus clouds to our left is a U-shaped valley, containing a wide meadow that arches up to the rocky cliffs of Mother Mountain. My eyes track down the canyon, noting the transition of grassland into thickening forest; at the junction of ridge and stream, three thousand feet below us, the Carbon River flows in its rocky bed. My attention snaps back to the proximate pasturage, intent on spotting bears, elk, or deer, but this garden is barren of large mammals.

From here the trail turns from north to east before arcing back to the north and descending into the heart of Cataract Valley. Stunning displays of flowers are coming fast and thick: bright yellow arrowhead groundsel, mauve Lewis monkey-flower, and amethyst larkspur smother every streamlet; lupines carpet the less boggy stretches of Seattle Park; thimbleberry, huckleberry, and salmonberry patches come and go. The pitch of the trail lessens, and I hope the camp will soon appear among the swampy meadows and mountain hemlock groves; however, no identifying sign materializes as we gravitate away from the open spaces.

The pathway creeps into a dark brooding forest and traverses along rocky bluffs that seem to harbor evil. Will man or beast ambush us? Silly, but I am wary, and by the time Cataract Camp is reached I am not relieved but instead am on guard. The immediate vicinity is inhabited by a dense stand of hemlock and silver fir, with a huckleberry understory. A steep, wooded hillside is behind us to the south and west, and a steep talus slope lies to the east beyond the camp. Seven tent pads are scattered under the big leaf maples, with two narrow brooks meandering through the grounds. It is not the campsites that bother me, for they are more than adequate, but instead it is the "feel" of the place. How does one account for queasiness, hairs up on end, and the desire to look repeatedly over your shoulder? A flannel shirt, hanging six feet up on a tree limb, seems to say, "We got one, and you're next."

"Whadda ya think?" Patrick asks tentatively. He is obviously as uncomfortable as I am, though neither of us will admit the truth.

I survey the area once again. "It's okay," I offer unconvincingly, "but I'd rather move on." Luckily, I do not have to beg him to continue.

"Let's go," he pronounces as he is pivoting toward the main trail.

Though there is only an hour before dark, we decide to take a chance that there is at least one site left at Carbon River Camp, and drop rapidly as if pursued by demons. The first mile weaves through the litter of a large timber windfall and then follows the bank of the brushy Cataract Creek drainage; I dreadfully anticipate a bear encounter in this gloomy morass at any moment. Mercurial strides vault me into an old-growth Douglas fir and western hemlock forest, with devil's club and ferns grabbing at my legs. A half mile farther and the Carbon River Trail is overtaken, then the camp is reached by turning left and rambling a hundred yards, crossing the bridge over Cataract Creek, and ascending twenty final yards.

Carbon River Camp is a series of cleared dirt patches in a dense thicket. Massive old-growth western hemlock tower overhead, with an occasional red cedar and Douglas fir to keep them company. Red alders are prominent along the waterways, while Pacific yews prevail at the drier campsite to create a dark, tangled, spooky arena. At ground level devil's club, salmonberry, oak ferns, and thimbleberry mix with huckleberry bushes to contrive an inviolable snarl.

The first two campsites are within thirty feet of the main trail, so we shun the remaining two that are somewhere up the hill in the impenetrable underbrush; even the toilet is hidden under the heavy shadows of yew and cedar trees, which I am hesitant to enter in the waning light. The first site is an easy pick, as it is accessible and bordered by a fortress of large fallen trees. Tonight I need the comfort of the human community. I hope a way-faring soul will arrive and bring good cheer.

Cataract Camp was so remote, here at least I feel in contact with mankind…just in case. Perhaps the essence of previous travelers lingers in the woods about us. Coal was discovered downstream in 1862, and hence the name Carbon River. In order to exploit the fossil fuel, and subsequently the fine sandstone, the Northern Pacific Railroad built a rail line to Wilkeson, and it was not long before enterprising rail men realized that a profit could be made in guiding voyagers to the vast realm of the volcano. From that cause, the Bailey Willis Trail was hacked out along the Carbon River, leading upstream to the land of ice and tundra.

Phantoms, sporting heavy flannel and wool clothing, parade by with walking sticks firmly in hand. Horses nicker quietly at unseen dangers lurking in the jungle, causing their riders to nervously wonder. Behind them, the road builders struggle between the steep mountain and unrestrained river to build an automobile passage. The roadway ended here at Cataract Creek in 1923, but its usefulness to motorized vehicles lasted only three years before the elements reclaimed the final three miles from Ipsut Campground. (*Ipsut* is the Chinook word for "hidden," which is a good description for the roadbed, as it is now only discernible as a broad hiking path.) Perhaps the asphalt we crossed three days ago at North Puyallup River will remain recognizable for what it was for longer than this lane; this avenue has been, and continues to be, a thoroughfare of human labor and joy. In the end, it is still wilderness, no matter how much we want it to be something less intimidating.

Neither Patrick nor I can explain our uneasiness in this corner of the mountain. What creature lurks in the dark forest: bear, lion, bigfoot, or crazed human? I keep the pepper spray and ice ax close at hand. Anxiety triggers primitive survival instincts and all my senses come alive. My ears strain, listening for twigs to crack, rhythmic splashing of water, or growling—echoes of a predator. It is peculiar to feel like a peasant in the food chain, instead of the king, but it is not original. Long-buried ancestral memories create macabre scenarios.

Bruce Chatwin, in *The Songlines*, discussed the concept of the "boogie man" as a real entity. Perhaps humans are afraid of the dark forest for a deeply ingrained purpose: survival. Some archeological sites suggest humans were the primary prey of some prehistoric beast. Chatwin describes Dinofelis as "…solidly built. It had straight, dagger-like killing teeth, midway in form between a sabre-tooth's and, say, the modern tiger's…it must have hunted by stealth…by night." Its range was the same as that of the fledgling human race; the cat's bones have been found in caves with the skulls of baboons and men, not antelope or deer.

Chatwin goes on to contemplate the theories of naturalist Bob Brain, including that Dinofelis and *Homo sapiens* inhabited the same caverns, the former ensconced deep in the bowels while the later bunched at the entrance. Blinded by nightfall, the primates would be picked away, one by one, by the stealthy feline. Chatwin: "Could it be, one is tempted to ask, that Dinofelis was Our Beast? A Beast set aside from all the other Avatars of Hell? The Arch Enemy who stalked us, stealthily and cunningly, wherever we went?" The lioness stalks us in the shadows.

Defenseless men who stray too far from the bipedal masses are vulnerable. Survival instincts are unveiled: back to the wall (of the cave), buddies back-to-back to prevent ambush, massed together, violently swinging our spears before us into the darkness to discourage attack.

At some point we got the better of our beast, perhaps by a mastery of fire or the collaboration with some animal with better night senses. The beast may have been purged from our reality, but not from our nightmares, as intuitions have been imprinted into the deepest-seated recesses of our brains by the blood of fallen, ancestral comrades. I should not ignore these feelings, but heed them, and find relative safety in the human community.

After supper, Patrick and I quickly huddle in the tent and zipper it tight, safe in our cave, and ready for defense from the fierce wildness outside. Cards are shuffled and thumbed absently in an attempt to distract ourselves. The wet socks, shorts, and shirts, hanging from the attic to dry, provide ample scent for the beasts of the woodland to identify this yellow-and-blue dome as the abode of *Homo sapiens*. I hope that is a good message to broadcast to omniscient noses.

Ultimately we doze off.

A Rumbling Mountain

In relation to the earth, we have been autistic for centuries. Only now have
we begun to listen with some attention and with a willingness to respond to
the earth's demands that we cease our industrial assault, that we abandon
our inner rage against the conditions of our earthly existence, that we renew
our human participation in the grand liturgy of the universe.

THOMAS BERRY, *THE DREAM OF THE EARTH*

Patrick and I did survive the night, slumbering placidly until roused by
the morning light announcing a gloriously beautiful day. The sky is robin's
egg blue; sunbeams streak over Crescent Mountain betwixt the massive
trees to draw steam out of our wet socks. Perhaps it is a residual side effect
of yesterday's unease, but we are anxious to exit this haunted woodland.
Hence, our gear is crammed into the packs swiftly and efficiently, in
between spoonfuls of oatmeal and swigs of steaming coffee, and when we
don the loads and hit the trail our spirits are instantly heightened.

Within a half mile we approach the suspension bridge over the wide,
boulder-strewn channel through which the milky white water of Carbon
River rumbles. This span is more dilapidated than the one arching over
Tahoma Creek; in fact, several planks are missing and others are cracked

and debilitated, groaning under the force of my weight. Yet the traverse is not intimidating with the river only twenty feet beneath my feet, and therefore I cross with relative ease of mind.

On the far side the route turns right, ascending on the East Carbon River Trail, initially under the cover of silver firs but then skirting along the base of a crumbling rock wall. I peek vigilantly to my left for any boulders that may teeter and topple from the overhanging cliff, although my consciousness is drawn upstream to my right, where a mass of ice flows down from the lofty mountain. Shortly, a vista point is reached, from which to fully focus ahead as the Carbon Glacier comes into full view for the first time. Patrick laughs as he takes a picture of a nearby sign. "I've got to show this to everyone back home."

Carbon Glacier
Danger
Falling rock, swift water,
Cave-ins. Stay away from
Glacier and river.

The glacier is alive! I have always held the opinion that glaciers are an amorphous mass of ponderous rock-grinding ice, "slow as a glacier,"

but here in front of me is a dynamo. Not only does a river emerge from its bowels, but also chunks of ice and boulders continually fall off its terminus.

Carbon Glacier has ebbed and flowed over the centuries with the fluctuations of the weather patterns. During the mini ice age (fourteenth century to 1850) all twenty-five named and the numerous other unnamed glaciers on Rainier advanced their farthest down the valleys since the time of the ice age. Subsequently, a leisurely backtrack turned into a more swift retreat after 1920, and by 1950 most glaciers had lost a quarter of their original length. Heavy snows then fueled a general expansion from 1950 to 1980, but now most glaciers are shrinking again.

Carbon Glacier is unique for several reasons. It is Rainier's thickest (705 feet in midbody) river of ice. Also, it is blanketed by a layer of black rock (the aftermath of a 1916 rockslide originating at distant Willis Wall) that insulates it from the assault of the sun, and has allowed it to forge down the mountain to this relatively low elevation. In the 1970s, hikers witnessed the glacier's march more graphically, as vegetation that was in the way got crushed by boulders rolling off the terminus.

I wonder what the future will hold for this dynamic entity? Perhaps manmade greenhouse gases will warm the planet. In that eventuality, the Carbon Glacier will be chased uphill, abdicating a smooth U-shaped valley and shallow, rocky tarns. Nearer the summit, compatriot glaciers and snowfields will evaporate, leaving behind the jagged skeleton of the mountain. Unclothed, the volcano may dance in its lightness— bulging, shedding rubble. In such temperate conditions trees would crawl skyward, as tundra succumbs to the heat. Nature abhors a vacuum. Incapable of constraining the rising magma, Rainier may explode riotously.

Undoubtedly the planet may react in self-defense, for it has the means to maintain its equilibrium. Warmer ground and surging lava may precipitate worldwide volcanic eruptions, with the accumulated offal darkening the atmosphere, and hence cooling the earth. If it overshoots a bit and the Earth's surface chills, so be it: ice sheets have enshrouded the Northern Hemisphere before. Permafrost would throttle the forests, and with their demise the opportunistic tundra would thrive, at least where the ice permitted it to do so. Though my actions may trigger the eventualities, I will not witness the repercussions. Yet for Earth it will all have

Marmot (above) and Pika (below)

My pulse hasn't diminished to that level, but with sweat dried, stomach sated, and muscles rested, I am ready to finish the final ascent into Moraine Park. Elk tracks smother the game trails that frequently crisscross our path, but the wapiti themselves remain ghosts. The distraction of searching for those animals makes the mile to Moraine Park glide by quickly.

"Wow! This looks like Alaska." The beauty of the meadowlands catches me off guard.

Moraine Park

Patrick agrees with my exclamation. "Bette played this down. I wonder if she was sick or something when she came through here?" Indeed, the guidebook speaks only cursorily of this plateau, which was recently freed from the cover of ice when a branch of the Carbon Glacier melted. Stretching before us is a spacious, rolling plain of low-growing bronze sedges, resembling the tundra of the Far North. Lupine greenery highlights the subalpine fir fringes. Within the steppe, miniscule ponds and serpentine streams create contrast in the landscape.

We abandon our packs on a large, flat rock and reconnoiter the surroundings. Precipitous Willis Wall looms before us; a fresh avalanche chute that we had viewed this morning is clearly demarcated. Here the mountain is not assembled in terraces, but leaps straight up into the stratosphere and is braced by two arms, in the form of ridges, extending to the northeast and northwest. I feel I am intrinsic to this biosphere; I breathe it in, and we become the same.

It is obvious that whistling marmots flourish here, and in fact one has dug a hole underneath the large flat boulder that is our current rocky perch. Intermittently he peeks out and squeals a warning. (I've read that marmot tunnel systems are quite elaborate and can extend for miles.) While we attempt to coax the critter out into the open with silence, a day hiker interrupts our scheme. The young man is here from Seattle and intends to complete a round trip from Carbon River to Mystic Lake and back, today. After a brief chat he resumes his trek.

Too soon, we hoist our packs for the final short steep climb over a ridge and down into the Mystic Lake Basin. During the descent we watch surreptitiously, while two hundred feet below us a large blacktail deer is startled from his bed by the day hiker. We soon pass the vacated scene, then go down a wooded hillside and emerge onto the grassy plain of Mystic Lake.

The terrain is initially characterized by thirty-foot-tall fir trees interspersed among knee-deep auburn sedges, and the turf varies from parched to boggy; wooden walkways are provided for dry footing where necessary. Within a half mile the lake presents itself, a real mountain gem. Witty old Ben Longmire thought he saw a whirlpool swirling in its waters, and hence dubbed it Mystic Lake. I do not notice any vortices, but I do appreciate that the shoreline is painted jade by well-watered grasses. Trees extend to the waterline only on the northern slope, while to the south a series of cold clear springs, lined by yellow monkey-flowers, emanate and flow briskly into the lake. We linger at this fountain long enough to refill our water bottles.

At the east side of the lake the trail descends abruptly toward the official campsite a quarter mile downhill. (Until the 1980s, people had camped up here on the shores, but that resulted in all the trees being stripped and the flowers and grasses being stomped down to the bare ground.) As it is still early in the day we unload our packs and walk around the north shore to locate the ranger cabin. Upon realizing it is a quarter mile up the hill, we resolve to visit the ranger after we have established our camp, but then even delay that endeavor in order to bask in the shoreside sun and monitor the luck of two fishermen who are plying the waters. All that I can identify in the crystal waters are inch-long trout minnows hugging the shallow shores, but I am convinced they avoid the deeper water where their cousins lurk, ready for an ambush. The older fish must also be wise, because I don't see any of them being caught by the fisherman. The anglers soon give up and fill their daypacks in preparation for the long hike out. I can empathize with their plight, as, in fact, many of my backpacking trips have been organized just to consummate a similar adventure; only with a backpack can you enjoy the sunset over such a sublime, but remote, pool.

Another pair of backpackers tramps past, rousing us to follow them down to camp, and by the time we arrive three of the seven sites are already occupied. However, a very fine spot, which is also the most elevated site under the dense cover of the silver fir, is still available for us. Before pitching the tent we explore the brushy clearing behind the camp; well-established game trails, undeniably bear highways, run through the shallow ravine. Fortunately there is a perfect bear-bagging tree nearby, and, together with the Park Service–furnished bear pole, it is more than adequate for our peace of mind against any nighttime marauders. After camp is secured we exchange the bulky boots for nimble tennis shoes, and retrace our steps to the lake with the goal of finding the ranger and changing our trip itinerary.

Rustic Mystic Lake Patrol Cabin is situated a quarter mile up the side trail north of the lake. Its rough-hewn log construction is similar to the cabins at Indian Henry's and Golden Lakes, but it has a more canted roof and is obviously a more recent vintage. The coarse pumice ground surrounding the structure is festooned with false hellebore, corn lily, paintbrush, and a multitude of deer tracks. From the covered wooden porch, the view is spectacular out over the lake basin to Mineral Mountain, and beyond to the precipitous northern slopes of Rainier itself. Pinned on the corkboard that leans against the cabin wall are updates and advisories for hikers: Don't drink the water, don't put food in your tent, don't approach bears, watch for falling rock around glaciers, etc. We lounge in the sunlight awhile waiting for the ranger's return, which does not come to fruition, so we'll have to try again later.

Back at camp, a quick glance reveals that all the campsites are now full. Four are taken by couples, one by a single guy, and the other by a group of two guys and a gal. The solo man is intent on talking with everyone, and his greetings resound through the forest. The banter establishes that the majority are circumnavigating the Northern Loop over a three- or four-day weekend.

Early in the evening the local ranger, Jeri, gathers us all together to review the campground rules. It is peculiar to be so instructed this far in the backcountry, but she is adamant in her warning that bears frequent this area, even toddling right through camp while people have been here; a large pile of bear crap near camp six corroborates her tale. So, no toiletry articles or food in the tents; every odorous item, including cooking utensils, should be bear-bagged. She also emphasizes that fires are not allowed, so cook only with gas stoves.

Jeri seems a bit eccentric and serious about her job, but perhaps there really are novices here. After her dissertation we ask how we can change our trip schedule, and she assures us this is quite a serious matter and requests that we come to the ranger cabin first thing in the morning, so that she can wire headquarters. Behind her aloofness, Jeri is well meaning, kind, and diligent.

After supper we revisit the bubbling, lakeside springs to fetch water, but while ambling along the southern edge of the lake we are distracted by a faint path, cutting up and over a fifteen-foot high knoll. I am curious about what lies on the other side, so I scramble to investigate. Beyond a fence of dense shrubby trees, the trail falls into a luxurious, bantam-sized, and quaint meadow with a crystal clear spring gurgling through its midst. Plopped in the middle of all is a bright yellow tent. How audacious! We are initially miffed that someone broke the rules and is camped here instead of at the campground, but that feeling soon switches into jealousy. I acknowledge that everyone can't camp here, or the lakeside would be decimated, but a rebel or two is okay. I just wish we were the rebel rousers. Back at the lake, we laud the fortune of the lucky person in the defiant shelter.

With water bottles topped off and the coffeepot replenished for the morning's caffeine requirements, we decide to stash our gear under the watch of a sentry fir tree and wander through the western pasturage in search of elk and bear. Barely removed from the lake's shores we encounter a twenty-something guy heading back toward the lake; his only burden is a fanny pack, hence we deduce he is camped near us.

A brief exchange of biographies establishes that Josh is on a weekend jaunt from Seattle. "I climbed Rainier a few weeks ago and just wanted to get away for some solitude," he further explains. I am always impressed by anyone who scales to the top of a formidable mountain; it does require thought-out preparation and a certain fortitude. The triumph also instills an unmistakable charisma into the conqueror.

"So do you do much backpacking?" Patrick asks him.

"No, not very often. I like to climb more than anything. How about you guys?"

"Well we like to backpack a lot," Patrick replies with emphasis. He truly does love the bonding with Nature that can only occur in the solitude of the backcountry. "Rainier is the longest trip for me so far, but we've done a lot of shorter trips."

Josh nods his head in approval, and appears curious to know more details. "So are you guys just getting started?"

"Actually this is our eighth day out," Patrick responds matter-of-factly.

"Wow." Perhaps this is mock surprise and he is just kidding with us, since by now we have rough beards and are malodorous to the noses of the civilized world, the trappings of a prolonged stint in the brush.

Patrick outlines our progress to this point, and further clarifies, "We planned to do the loop in fourteen days, but we're thinking about changing our permit to do it in thirteen."

By now I can't restrain my curiosity about his alpine adventure. It is one thing to peruse historical accounts but is quite different, and more enthralling, to be entertained by a first-hand account—though no facsimile is equal to the original experience. With that notion in mind I redirect the conversation. "So what was it like to climb Rainier?"

Josh is easy-going and animated but not boisterous, and for that reason I believe that his account is not exaggerated. "Actually, it's not that technical or anything. You get up early from Muir Camp and are to the summit by early morning. But it can still be dangerous. I mean, I few weeks before I went up, some guy died up there."

"Really, we didn't hear anything about that," I utter with surprise. There had been no mention of the accident at the Hiker/Climber Center; both Patrick and I are leaning forward, awaiting more details.

What little he knew apparently was garnered from other climbers. "Yeah, I guess the guy had climbed Everest and everything."

"How ironic to die here, on a mountain half that tall." I am sorrowful for the unfortunate fellow, he having trekked to the far ends of the Earth only to inadvertently stumble to his demise in the backyard. Familiarity and aplomb engender nonchalance. My drive to work along the same route is repeated until it is perfunctory, done in a trance, concentration drifting away at the critical moment when it is imperatively required to resolve an unanticipated deviation. Perhaps the unfortunate fellow was stepping in a reminiscent fog, but then again, he may have been fully extant and it was just his fate.

"You never know. I guess he just caught his crampons on the ice and tumbled into a crevasse. Just like that," Josh gestures with his hands dropping to the earth.

"What a way to go," I murmur. No one will ever know the truth of that moment; it exhorts consideration of my own destiny.

Josh insinuates that he is contemplating analogous sentiments. "Did you guys ever read the book—let me think what's it called—*Touching the Void*, I think."

"What's it about?" Patrick encourages.

"It's about this hardcore climber who falls off a cliff. He fell two thousand feet or something but still survived. I guess he was all banged up and had to lay there on the edge of a crevasse for quite a while, until his climbing partner could go get help. It happened somewhere down in South America."

"That would suck," Patrick retorts with a slightly disturbed tone.

"No kidding! In the book he talks about thinking about dying, and trying to rationalize climbing and everything. But it's way cool. You should read it," Josh concludes earnestly; it's his favorite book.

"We'll have to look that one up. I'm sure Barnes and Noble would carry it in the outdoors section." It does sound interesting.

Patrick steers the discussion to one of our favorite books. "Have you ever read *Into the Wild*?"

"Never heard of it. Is it about climbing?"

"No. It's kinda hard to explain, but basically it's about this guy—Chris McCandless—who gives up everything, but ends up dying in the woods." Josh appears perplexed. It is difficult to explicate the rationale for someone discarding all worldly possessions to roam the underground of America.

"Does he get injured somehow?"

Patrick attempts to clarify the gist of the book. "Not really. I guess he was really smart and from an upper-middle-class family, even went to college, but he apparently cracked or something. Gave up all his possessions and disappeared. He didn't even try to contact his family again." McCandless was enraptured with an archetypal existence. Shaped by paradigms devoid of pragmatism, "living off the land," and such.

"Man, I could never do that. Sometimes I think about disappearing for a while, but I couldn't abandon my family," Josh states with conviction.

It is an intriguing saga, quite contrary to that which we would choose, and it seems Josh is tantalized as I continue the tale. "So he abandoned his car, 'cause it got stuck, gave his money away to charity, and just hitchhiked his way around the country, on the West Coast mainly."

"Kinda weird." Josh shakes his head negatively, shuffling his weight from leg to leg uneasily.

"Yeah, then he went up to Alaska and hiked into the backcountry until he found this abandoned bus, where he stayed for six months or so," I explain. McCandless's big adventure in the outdoors was along a quasi-developed roadway within fifteen miles or so of the hardtop, not in the remote bush. His preparations were purely philosophical. In fact, a sympathetic Alaskan who conveyed the hitchhiker to the trailhead also equipped the sojourner with warm clothing and waterproof boots. Mind you, this was March in the heart of Alaska.

"So how did he die?"

"Well, he didn't get attacked by any animal, but he confused some poison plant for an edible one and it slowly weakened him to the point he couldn't walk. The sickest thing is that he kept this journal and wrote about slowly dwindling away," Patrick elaborates on the ghastly details.

Josh obviously disbelieves that anyone would go into the wild so unprepared, but I can't comprehend why he didn't do more to help himself. "What I don't understand is how he could just hang out there for all that time, without really trying to get out. I guess he tried to leave once, but the river was too flooded to cross, so he returned to the bus and just hung out until he died."

"Stupid!" Josh interjects perturbably.

"I know. If it were me I would have hiked upstream until the stream got small enough to cross, even if it took weeks," I exclaim with a hint of disgust in my voice. "Even worse, I guess there was this metal cable spanning the river a half mile down from where he tried to cross. He could have shimmied his way across and got back to the main road."

"I don't get it either," he agrees.

"It makes me think that he was suicidal." Indeed, from a distance it looks as though he was consigned to his fate.

"Probably."

"The book was comparing him to other guys who went into the wild to find themselves. Maybe he would have been a Muir if he had survived," Patrick adds.

"Maybe. But I always think of Muir as being prepared and understanding the environment. He was able to survive because of his outdoor skills and knowledge of plants and such," I argue.

"I agree. For McCandless to just go into the woods with no survival skills whatsoever is pie-in-the-sky. A dreamer." Patrick and I have discussed this topic before and are in agreement that the artistic constitution must be counterbalanced by the practical.

I expound further on that concept. "Yeah, it wasn't like he was trying to understand the world around him, but just hoping to survive by the grace of God. Like tempting death."

"*Into the Wild*, huh. I'll have to look that one up," Josh declares. We reassure him that it is a worthwhile read.

After a momentary pause, during which we all survey the mountains, Patrick is inquisitive about how Josh came to be here. "So are you here by yourself?"

"Yeah, my girlfriend dropped me off and will be coming back on Sunday to pick me up. I don't really have a plan. Just wandering around," Josh elucidates.

"That's the best way sometimes," Patrick opines. "So she doesn't make a big deal about you doing this without her?"

After a chuckle Josh explains, with a mischievous twinkle in his eye, "No, she's not really into the outdoors. I think she looks forward to me leaving so she can go shopping." We all snicker sagaciously.

"That's so cool, that she doesn't get all bent out of shape when you want to do something like this. Not everyone is that generous." Patrick is obviously impressed that a couple could have such a trusting relationship. "Not everyone likes the same things, and it's very cool that you guys allow each other room to do your own thing."

"Well, we still have a lot of fun together and do a lot together too." Josh is impelled to clarify his high level of devotion to her. "Just, every once in a while, I need my space and I'm lucky that she lets me have it."

"Yeah, not everyone is so lucky," Patrick concurs stolidly.

"Well I've got to make dinner before it gets too late." Josh abruptly ends the conversation and heads over to the spring to purify water for his supper.

Patrick and I continue through the grassland until we reach the forest boundary. No animals. We are a bit disappointed, but the rosy twilight reflected by the snowy mountainside is a wondrous consolation. Stupendous! After eight days of wilderness seasoning, we are no longer seeking to fulfill expectations, but go forth attentively. The wilderness does not submit to our solicitations, but instead we glissade through it like an interactive amusement park ride.

Elbowing Patrick in the side, I make a wager with him about Josh. "Hey, I bet he's the one in that hidden tent near the lake."

"You think?"

"Yeah." He certainly would fit the personality profile. We both glance inconspicuously across the lake to spy on Josh, who by now has gathered up his belongings and is shuffling beside the south shore of the lake. When Josh casually halts in front of the crude path to the illegal campsite, and then turns to behold the lake, I glance at Patrick triumphantly. Josh's head slowly rotates right then left, ensuring the coast is clear, and then he suddenly pivots, bounds up the hill and down out of sight to his yellow nylon lair.

I spit out boastfully, "See, I thought it would be him."

"Good for him," Patrick replies with a congenial tone.

"Yeah, good for him," I echo. "I hope the ranger doesn't harass him."

"That's right. Jeri seems pretty strict about the rules of camping here," Patrick snickers. We both have a good laugh imaging the confrontation: "live by the rules" and "rules are meant to be broken" collide. With a light heart we circle back to camp.

By now the encampment has quieted considerably. Hushed conversation and restrained laughter float to my ears. In the darkness, I throw together the cornbread mix, but it takes forever to bake and my negligence results in it being mostly burned. After nibbling the soft tasty center, the remainder is tossed in the bags that are bound for the bear pole. I hope the neighborhood bruin isn't enticed to visit us by the doughy aroma; however, quite candidly, I am not that worried and fall asleep pronto.

A resounding crack followed by a reverberation, like thunder, jolts me out of my slumber. "Really a thunderstorm?" I mumble out loud in a dazed state. I am puzzled how a tranquil, starry night could transform so quickly into a turbulent, stormy midnight. Soon I can discern the distinctive cacophony of boulders ricocheting downhill and the grating of skidding gravel. It sounds so close that initially I fear that we are about to be buried alive in an avalanche, but after the adrenaline abates from my veins,

I realize that the clamor emanates from the distant glacier and volcano. We're not in immediate peril. Through the still night air the mountain continually rumbles.

I wonder why so much energy is utilized to assemble Mount Rainier just to have wind and rain gradually reduce it to rubble. Indeed, nothing is sanctified. A rose seems so flawless, yet it metamorphoses into a hip that falls to the ground to be composted, only to arise again in a subsequent generation. Nature is indeed very efficient in using and reusing its components, but why does it never desist and proclaim, "This rose is so impeccable that I will grant it immortality"? Albeit, the concept of imperishability is repulsive to me: stagnant, insipid, apathetic, paralyzed, timid.

Mount Rainier is magnificent, sporting its cloak of ice, forest, animals, and insects, but it is mortal. In the darkness I envision the entire state of Washington as it was fifty million years ago: flat swampland (the source of the sandstone and coal deposits now mined near Rainier). Deep under the ocean a series of volcanic eruptions disturbs the horizon, creating offshore islands that will be the substance of the Ohanapecosh Formation (now east of Rainier). Subsequent eruptions form the Stevens Ridge and Fifes Peak Formation, leading up to twelve million years ago when molten rock pushes up through to form the Tatoosh Pluto, which now includes Eagle Peak south of Rainier. After that the Cascade Range gradually rose. It all seems like a bubbling stew, with solid rock springing out of the muck. Mount Rainier, as we now know it, did not yet exist. Then one million years ago molten lava oozes up through a crack in the Earth's crust to conceive proto-Rainier. Subsequent outbursts from two satellite cones, Echo Rock and Observation Rock, augment the mound, followed by thick pumice deposition on the eastern aspect of the volcano until thirty thousand years ago. Magma surges continue episodically up through the central conduit system and out the ever-changing summit crater. Tremendous explosions of ash and rock alternate with interludes of relative calm, when only the whisper of steam melting cavities in the icy cap insinuates the magnitude of the furor within.

Mount Rainier is a typical composite volcano—her flanks are sheer. During the ice age, glaciers shrouded the landscape from the young mountain to the sea. Following the thaw fifteen thousand years ago the peak retained its private icebox, so as to nurture her myriad rivers. By six thousand years ago, Mount Rainier, at sixteen thousand feet tall, towered above the Cascades, but she is an impermanent pile of rocks rotting at the core; steam and chemical-laden gases weaken her innards.

Approximately 5,040 years ago some trigger set in motion the collapse of the top two thousand feet of the mountain, with the enormous volume of runaway rubble thundering all the way to Puget Sound in a calamity known as the Osceola Mudflow. Just how this could happen relates back to the eroding interior. Whether it was an earthquake or not we will never know, but once the soft insides were jiggled into liquid clay the slurry carried away large blocks of the more solid exterior shell. Enormous slabs were ferried down the White River and ultimately deposited, where they can still be seen as large streamside mounds today. The bulk of the deluge reached Puget Sound in less than four hours, thrusting the shoreline out several miles; the towns of Kent, Sumner, Auburn, and Puyallup are built on the marooned sediment of pebbles, rocks, and sand.

The devastated Mount Rainier was disfigured with a huge east-facing amphitheater resembling present-day Mount St. Helens. However, eruptions have subsequently patched the wound and even spawned a second crater on the summit. The elder cone is Liberty Cap and the younger is Point Success, and where they overlap, at the Columbia Crest, the mountain peaks at 14,411 feet. I wonder if the mountain is being whittled away in midlife or yet has some volatile growing pains to experience?

In the grand scheme of the universe Rainier has had but a temperamental, transient presence. A million years hence only a remnant mound will abide, akin to a star that coalesces for a billion years before a detonation spews its pulverized residue throughout the cosmos. Even the universe itself may have been engendered only to fizzle and collapse in exhaustion.

Humans are conceived and nurtured, reach maturity, and then wither away into the soil. Cursorily, the modus operandi of summarily destroying that which tremendous resources were expended upon to build appears wasteful. Nonetheless, from the forest humus fledgling beings arise. All carbon, oxygen, nitrogen, and iron, fundamental to vitality, are liberated from their creator when the heart of a star bursts. All entities are born, bloom, sow, and expire…including the universe.

If physical subsistence perpetually transforms to ameliorate, what about the metaphysical—my soul? The water and nutrients that are requisite to assemble an adult body are naught in comparison to the exertion wielded in nurturing a soul. From childhood to the grave, we all learn what is right and wrong, how to share, care, and love. We continually search for that which instills vivacity, fulfillment, and serenity; it is difficult to believe that all is lost when we die. Surely the soul assimilates the lifetime of lessons when it departs the material plane, like the amassed genome of a rose seed; the soul is a kernel ready to sprout into another generation.

As the mountain rumbles in the night, I am adrift in supposition. What is driving this madness? Why such energetic growth going headlong into destruction? Why do I spend so much time on personal improvement only to forfeit it all in death? Is this God's blueprint for existence? The universe is not a perpetual motion machine repeating the same cycle unfailingly, but it alters with each loop.

I like to believe that God has planted his garden and tends it with passion. Every spring a new generation of flower, human, star, universe, and soul sprouts; cross-pollinates in the maturity of summer; bares a seed, child, supernova, black hole, and existential projection in autumn; and fertilizes the soil for the next progeny in winter. God lovingly cultivates all epochs in quest of impeccable beauty. Seemingly improvident destruction is, in reality, a stepping-stone toward perfection.

So in the still, darkness of the night, I listen to life cycling through Rainier. My body will not behold the voyage completed, but my soul might.

Sunrise

A virtuous man when alone loves the quiet of the mountains. A wise man in nature enjoys the purity of water. One must not be suspicious of the fool who takes pleasure in mountains and streams. But rather measure how well he sharpens his spirit by them.

MURO MUSEK, AS QUOTED IN *TEMPLE WILDERNESS*

The dawn's first light stirs the air, muting the mountain's rumbles. Patrick and I arise early to enjoy a cup of coffee before heading up the hill to Jeri's cabin, with the purpose of eliminating the layover day scheduled for Berkeley Park two days hence. It's not that we're growing weary of the wilderness—in fact we both feel totally relaxed and at peace—but it's more the momentum of it all; a body in motion tends to stay in motion. With lighter packs and well-conditioned legs, there is no need for a day of rest. Also, the side trip to Grand Park, which sounded so spectacular at home, now seems like an illicit affair; we resolve to stay with our Wonderland Trail lover.

Even though we are unencumbered by packs, the short climb up the steep incline to the patrol cabin makes me a bit winded and light-headed. I've always found that the first mile of any day is the worst; after that my body is warmed up, lungs and heart primed for action. On the way to the lake we follow a couple from camp, who appear determined and mechanical, with their bodies clad in all the newest Capilene, Gore-Tex, and fleece, grasping ski pole–style walking sticks in either hand, which click-clack against the ground as they parade along. "Quite the trendy couple," Patrick quips light-heartedly. "Ready for an REI photo shoot." I have the impression that they are marching through the wilderness, instead of blending in and opening up their souls to it.

At the lakeshore the stylish pair strides purposefully around the left bank, while we turn right and finish the ascent to the ranger cabin. Jeri responds to our knock on the front door by emerging onto the porch to share the stunning panorama of Mount Rainier towering over Mystic Lake. She points to Mineral Mountain, on the southeast corner of the lake, and notes that rangers have counted as many as thirty-seven goats there at one time. With an exasperated sigh she grumbles that she rarely sees wildlife, despite dwelling here from June to October; the bear always has run off the trail, the elk sprinted into the woods, and the goat clambered around the mountain bluff, just before she arrives. Chitchat establishes that she is a volunteer, and as such can abide here for as long as the weather allows, unlike the ranger couple we had met near Tahoma Bridge who are paid employees and depart in September when the money runs out.

The three of us sit down on the front steps, as Jeri radios Longmire on her military style walkie-talkie. I envision the retired gentlemen at the Hiker Center struggling to hear the message embedded in the overwhelming static, while simultaneously trying to figure out how to get the computer to do what he wants it to do. After several repetitions, and the aid of a third-party walkie-talkie intermediary, we successfully change our coming destinations to be Sunrise, Summerland, Indian Bar, Nickel Creek, and the car; at Indian Bar we will have the group site, for the reason that all the individual spots are already reserved. With a smile of satisfaction, we wish Jeri well then return to camp to have breakfast, pack up, and go.

The route to Sunrise initially descends under forest cover, and in the process fords several headwater streams that feed into the West Fork of the White River. The threesome from camp passes by, while we pause to filter water. They are talking so loudly and walking so quickly that I wonder if they are afraid to be out here in the wilds. It also flashes into my consciousness what a scandal this young woman would have created in 1890—the year Fay Fuller reached the summit of Rainier.

As a schoolteacher in nearby Yelm, Fay bade Van Trump himself to lecture to her pupils on two separate occasions. Perhaps the requests were more for her indulgence, considering "his enthusiasm made me want to go up." No adequate climbing gear existed for her at that time, because such ventures were considered inappropriate for women in the Victorian era, but, not to be deterred, Fay wore "heavy flannels, woolen hose, warm mittens and goggles, blackened my face with charcoal to modify the sun's glare." With an old shovel handle serving as her alpenstock, she indeed topped the peak. If the story ended there she may have been regarded as a heroine, but like Van Trump and Stevens before her, she was forced to huddle in an ice cave to survive a stormy night—unchaperoned—with four men. How scandalous!

Once the chattering trio is out of ear and eyeshot, we resume the descent to the main channel of the West Fork of the White River. The smooth stones of the streambed are high and dry, due to the fact that the water has been diverted, by fallen logs, through the midst of the woodland. The unrestrained whitewater continues to tug at the roots of those trees still standing in its path, and rip away considerable chunks of the slope that we are walking along. We cautiously skirt along the edge of an unstable thirty-foot-tall embankment, occasionally kicking loose gravel that bounds down into the water to our left. Eventually we cross the river itself by way of two parallel logs on which a level tread has been cut, which is much easier than we had expected from the guidebook description.

Curving around another hillock we reach the terminal moraine of the receding Winthrop Glacier. Stunted Douglas and silver fir toil to survive in the mammoth pile of gravel and boulders; the footpath twists and turns among the red, gray, and black rocks. Removed from the umbrella of the woodland the air temperature instantly jumps up ten degrees and the direct sunlight bakes my face. In a half mile we breach Winthrop Creek via a large log, after which we stop for a view of Garda Falls plummeting down through the hemlock forest to our left. The cool mist wafting through the trees is soothing to my chapped skin, but we hesitate only briefly before beginning our ascent to Skyscraper Pass.

The trio observed this morning is soon overtaken, as they labor amid the serviceberry and alder brush alongside Winthrop Glacier. They have spread apart, and are huffing and puffing independently during the climb, and in their competition engender frustration, because they will not let us pass. By now our legs are strong, on account of our training and decreased weight of our packs, allowing us to elevate with vigor. Finally they concede and we spring up the incline past them.

The trail rises, at times abruptly, through a thick stand of western hemlock and Douglas fir, similar to that explored on the western shoulder of Rainier. A distant, low rumble announces the appearance of Granite Creek, but it teases us only for another half mile before we finally sit by its clear, tumbling waters. By now spruce and subalpine fir are predominate in the canopy; where they relinquish control of the sunbeams, wet meadows and seeping springs splash in an intense emerald coloration. Reaping the benefits of the moisture and compost in the bogs are stout stalks of parsnip, the pervasive Lewis monkey-flower, and vibrant yellow glacier lilies.

Poor Patrick has a stomachache, probably from too much coffee, and while he digs out the Rolaids I filter water from this invigorating, mossy-stone-lined, ten-foot-wide brook. Then I exchange my ponderous leather boots for comfortable tennis shoes in which to jaunt around the area. After spreading my perspiration soaked socks out to dry in a patch of sunshine, I wander around, including an investigation of the small campsite perched twenty feet up the bank. By the time I return Patrick is already feeling better, and is fervent to dispatch the final rise to Skyscraper Pass.

In three-quarters of a mile the trail enters a sparsely treed subalpine meadow, and by the mile mark leaves the forest altogether. Though there are rare subalpine firs, twisted into obscene caricatures by the fierce winds; these krummholz may be hundreds of years old, but nonetheless their trunks are no thicker than my wrist. Each sports a skirt of stout boughs to keep the gales from lifting them by the waist and toppling them; where the limbs grope the earth, roots sprout and a clone is born. We leave the last of these close-knit families and surge forward to the incredible plateau of Skyscraper Pass.

From this tremendous vantage point there is an unobstructed view across the gently sloping ridge and far beyond. Tiny Mystic Lake is nestled in the trees back to our left, with accompanying Mineral Mountain and Old Desolate Peak seeming inconsequential, considering their tops are now at eye level. Behind us, majestic Rainier is luminous in the cloudless sky, and when I pivot 180 degrees, the air is so crystal clear that the details of distant Mount Baker are readily discernible. Upon reaching the penultimate crest itself, we can easily trace the distinct snaking track of the pathway to Sunrise, as it winds counterclockwise through the stunning bowl of Berkeley Park, which is lined with apple green, vivacious meadows.

It is barely three and a half miles from this memorable viewpoint to the parking lots of Sunrise; so many day hikers have made this their ultimate destination. A procession of young athletes sporting baseball caps and senior citizens crowned with wide-brimmed straw hats stroll up and feast their eyes on the grand sight, often producing a camera from their fanny packs to document the occasion. Hikers are seemingly everywhere, on and off the trail. I overhear the conversations of some of those who wander near, and I have to chuckle at those who trek so far in quest of this stunning vista but only discuss their tuna fish sandwich and how exceptional the macaroni salad was last night.

The comedy aside, I long for the wildness of the backcountry. Scanning down the bowl, I distinguish the landmarks of the forest interspersed with meadow denoting the location of Berkeley Park Camp. Then I realize with satisfaction (because we altered our schedule) that if we were lodged there we would have had to endure a cavalcade of people tromping through and picnicking at the camp, so perhaps it wouldn't have been such a good layover spot after all.

From a distance Skyscraper Pass appears to be barren rock, but now that I am here I am astounded by the diversity at my feet. There are a wider variety of flowers here than at any other trailside environ so far, and Patrick and I compete to see who can compose the most impressive picture. Short white yarrow prospers further down the slope, in the relative protection of the dwarf subalpine firs; patches of cinquefoils thrust their bright yellow petals up into the air, like patches of sunshine; there are diminutive Magenta Paintbrushes, tiny silvery alpine lupines, drooping sky-blue harebells, red tinged stonecrops, and bright red berries on ground-hugging kinnikinnick.

The afternoon dissolves effortlessly while sitting in the intense sunshine, with the procession of human interlopers transforming into a mere illusion in my transcendental state. To the south, Mount Rainier shimmers in the heat waves rising from its rocky flanks. To the north, the large green lake of Grand Park sits enticingly just out of reach. We had thought we would day hike to it on our layover day, but not now, because it would feel like I was abandoning the Wonderland Trail if I left its tread for even a couple of miles. To not run through the meadows of Grand Park at this time is not depravation, but is a dream for the future. Patrick and I promise each other that someday we will come back, and hike the Northern Loop past Grand Park to Yellowstone Cliffs and the Carbon River asunder. Reluctantly, we drift back to our gear and prepare to move on, or else risk hiking in the dark.

Dan climbing past Burroughs Mountain with Mount Rainier in the distance

The trail sweeps down, around, then up the cirque at the head of Berkeley Park, with the tread underfoot shifting from fertile dirt to a moonscape of muted reddish-brown pumice. Splashes of bright red and dull yellow knotweed break the monotony. In shielded crevices, speedwell raise their dainty, cobalt blue flowers to the heavens, with their long white stamens resembling eyelashes batting at the sun.

Two miles later we come to the Frozen Lake Trail junction and examine the tiny ice-covered lake, which is blockaded by a chain-link fence to keep out the masses; there are plenty of people here now. Multitudes of blue jean–clad tourists straggle along the trail from their automobiles. I can hear Spanish, German, and Arabic languages being spoken, in addition to the prevalent English. Most folks linger, unsure of their next step. (The majority return from hence they came.) A confounding factor is that the shortcut that would normally permit a half-mile drop to Sunrise Camp and that day hikers use to complete a scenic loop is closed because of a sizable snowbank; it would be quite a slippery, and potentially dangerous, glissade down the steep hillside. We seriously consider boot-skiing off-limits or looping southwest along the Burroughs Mountain Trail, though the sign suggests that trail might be impassable also, before we come to a consensus that following the well-worn path to Sunrise would be the prudent plan of action.

Sunrise is a spacious natural amphitheater positioned on the northeast corner of Mount Rainier, and is the highest point on the mountain that can be reached by car. However, it has been a stage for human drama long before the internal combustion engine sputtered its poison gas into the crystalline air. While surveying the arena for the best route to camp I can't help but ponder about the costumes that Sunrise has worn over the centuries. My mind cleanses the slopes of people, fences, trails, and buildings, thereby regressing the mountain back to its tumultuous childhood, the youthful behemoth churning, writhing, and rising into the atmosphere. Glaciers cloak its shoulders then melt away, landslides scrape its flesh, and rain washes away the rounded dome. Fresh green grass and fir boughs sooth Tacoma's wounds.

Like flipping photographs through my hands, I can envisage the impetuous plays of humanity; "Sunrise" has had a lot of names. The first image is one depicting elk, bear, deer, and goats nibbling complacently on the supple grasses. The Native Americans cautiously wander onto the slumbering giant, in pursuit of the fruits it bears. Realizing what a wonderful place this is they decide to make it a regular stop, whenever the snow will permit access, and by the time white man arrives, this is the favorite summering ground for the Yakama sub-chief Owhi. I try to imagine his residence among the other brush shelters down in the meadow. Women picking berries and drying medicinal herbs; men hunting beasts reverently; ponies grazing in the meadows. All is not work, for there is ample time for horse racing, games, courting, and laughter. This is "Me-yah-ah Pah," the Place of the Chief, which the white man subsequently called Yakima Park.

Sunrise

The album flips another page to reveal early white settlers grazing their sheep on the gentle slopes. The Yakama have long since been chased onto reservations or died of European diseases. The next page jumps ahead to "Sunrise." The current name came into vogue in 1931, when a multipurpose log and stone structure was built here, behind which 215 housekeeping cabins provided basic shelter for adventurous tourists—Sunrise had become a short-term destination, and no longer a home. After World War II the tents were dismantled one by one and the meadow relegated to a scarred picnic ground.

My inner vision snaps forward to that caressing my retinas currently. There are several substantial wood and rock structures at the far end of the meadow, but the picnic ground and its access road, which originated from the currently used parking lot in the distance, have been torn up. All that remains are grass-seeded dirt byways; a photograph taken a decade in the future will document these paths being swallowed up by the living meadow. What will the image be a century or two from now? More or fewer human developments, or perhaps the volcano will wipe the canvass clean and inaugurate a new painting.

With our debate concluded, we embark on the mile and a half loop down through Sunrise. The trail initially follows a ridgeline on which wind-sculpted whitebark pine and Engelmann spruce thrives; hugging the ground are goldenrod, penstemon, golden fleabane, alpine lupine, cinquefoil, buckwheat, and spreading phlox.

As we cross the final meadow before entering the developed sector, we happen upon an assembly of twenty tourists listening intensely to the presentation given by a park ranger on the topic of the local wildlife. Tramping through their midst I swear I overhear a little girl ask her mother, "What are they?" as if we are some unidentified beasts. Her mother whispers with slight trepidation, "They're backpackers."

"Did you see the kids gawking at us?" Patrick speaks softly, after we have passed them. "I just wanted to roar as loud as I could at them." After scrutinizing our heavy beards and sweaty skin caked with dust, we both burst out laughing. I'm sure we smell and look like barbarians.

The three-story, natural wood-sided Visitors Center is unfortunately closed, as is the ranger station. In fact, most folks here are stashing their gear and evacuating the parking lot to return to their warm homes. It is rather funny how people stare at us like we're not human, especially the children, but we are far from being jealous of them. Patrick and I are happy to remain on the fringes of civilization and are not ready to go back to its distractions yet; the energy it projects feels negative and uninviting.

There are a few positive aspects to this intersection with the mechanized world, however. Patrick takes the opportunity to call his mother, and she reports that the dogs are fine and everyone is well there, and Patrick was happy to relay that we also are doing well and having a wonderful journey. The parties on either side of the telephone line are comforted by the progress reports. The communications system is not the only luxury we take advantage of at Sunrise, because, for the first time since Longmire, we can wash up with running water from a spigot over a sink, though with the residual stench, I would not want to be the fellow that follows us. Best of all, we locate a garbage can to dump our trash, and Patrick is elated to unload the large ballast of gorp that he has been carrying untouched these many days. We were sure we would be eating it with gusto, but it looks less appetizing with every passing moment. Rejoice! Rejoice! The packs are becoming lighter!

With the completion of those chores we realize that the sun has fallen behind the mountain, and so we race the last mile to the campsite. Where it follows the perimeter of the ridge that we will descend to the White

River tomorrow, the trail is lined by wandering daisies and mountain arnica. However, Sunrise Camp is the least scenic spot at which we have pitched our tent to this point, by virtue of it being situated along the previously noted, abandoned road and picnic area that are being transformed back into wilderness. Unfortunately, it is so close to Sunrise that hikers frequently wander through camp, giving me the impression that I am in someone's backyard.

Despite its lack of seclusion the clearing we have chosen is actually quite nice, with an ample level surface set within a copse of twenty-foot-high subalpine firs. Down the slope a hundred yards behind us is shallow, unpretentious Shadow Lake, which serves as our water source. Only two other groups are camped here, the closest being a pair of retired men residing at the site next to ours.

With post-prandial cups of hot spiced cider in hand, Patrick and I decide to get acquainted with our neighbors. Both are about six feet tall, with weathered, tanned skin and slightly overweight frames; their noses are rather distinctive, with one being hooked and the other Romanesque. The funny thing is that even after talking with them for ten minutes or so, we never found out their names. What we know is that one of them is from New York State and the other is from Washington State, both are retired and desert their wives once a year to link up for a backpacking trip, with this year's excursion being a ten-day circuit around Mount Rainier.

As best I can piece together, they are packing light by resupplying at three different locations and carrying only a small emergency tent. Their campsite is rather spartan, with two sleeping bags laid out on sheets of clear plastic, a pair of antiquated external frame backpacks reclining against a fallen log, and a small gas backpacking stove heating up water for tea and to rehydrate a packet of freeze-dried food. There is no semblance of an attempt to bear bag, so I assume they plan to fight off the bruins if confronted.

It is obvious that they want the conversation to end, so Patrick and I retreat to our tent site. After a foray to the lake to procure water for the morning, we retire to the tent to play cards and read. In the stillness of the crisp night air I can hear the old guys talking quietly, their voices low and mellow so that I can't quite comprehend them, which is just as well with me, though it does give the impression of plotting.

"They give me the creeps," Patrick mutters, while drawing a card to play in our game of three thirteen. We are both sprawled out, side-lying on the sleeping bags, with the deck of playing cards between us.

I peer over my hand with a quizzical expression. "What do you mean?"

Patrick discards and hesitates before he replies. "I don't know." He shrugs his shoulders somewhat embarrassed. "They just make me uncomfortable. Maybe I'm just being paranoid, but there's something peculiar about them." This last declaration is resolute, but he still avoids my eye contact.

"They weren't very talkative," I offer. "Maybe they have something to hide." Why is it that strangers are both exotic and dreaded? Is our paranoia another primitive instinct to be heeded? Humankind required diversity to evolve and succeed, but not to perish carelessly in some Darwinian "survival of the fittest" battle.

Patrick runs with the villainous concept. "Yeah, they're probably convicts, like robbers and murderers. Who would look for them here? You know, they could just drift around the mountain for a few weeks until everyone thought they had left the area, then sneak back out under cover of darkness." He is pleased with his theory, and nods convincingly with a wry smile; I'm not sure if I should take him seriously or not.

I draw a card, analyze my hand, and discard, then snicker, "You are paranoid."

Patrick ignores our game and sets his cards on the sleeping bag upon which we are stretched. Initially he maintains a solemn countenance, but then he chortles, attempting not to laugh too loudly or else the fellows next door will hear him. Between titters he blurts out, "Well you never know. They were just so evasive."

"Well some people probably think the same about us. Especially when we are just starting out, and want to unwind. Talking to others is the last thing you want to do." Strangely, I feel a need to defend them.

"Yeah, maybe," Patrick acquiesces. "But I swear they had a gun by their pack."

"I didn't see that," I declare doubtfully. "But some people are nervous about the bears. You know, they want their 'protection.'" Certainly we have been oft maligned for not toting a pistol.

"Bears...or people maybe." Patrick insinuates that they are up to no good. "Just don't be surprised if you hear them shuffling about the tent in the middle of the night," he concludes with an "I warned you" tone.

We continue to eavesdrop on their muffled voices, intermingled with the tinny sound of metal spoon on a metal pot, issuing from their campsite. Are they hiding from some mysterious past? My inner voice ponders that question, and on another level asks, why should I fear the mysterious and unknown?

Summerland

Though I do not expect that I shall be reborn directly as a crocus, I know that one day my atoms will inhabit a bacterium here, a diatom there, a nematode or a flagellate—even a crayfish or a sea cucumber. I will be here, in myriad forms, for as long as there are forms of life on earth. I have always been here, and with a certain effort of will, I can sometimes remember.

JOHN A. LIVINGSTON, *ONE COSMIC INSTANT: A NATURAL HISTORY OF HUMAN ARROGANCE*

Muffled baritone voices mix with the metallic din of spoon on plate to announce the arrival of a new day. The grizzled chaps are breaking camp in the vague predawn light. Their respectful intonations and the faint ruffle of nylon are actually calming, not menacing—like listening to your grandfather rustling with the coffeemaker in the kitchen, while you're still snug in bed. By the time I muster the energy to launch myself out of the tent, they are already prepared to depart. My motivation was not to see them off, but instead to witness the eastern horizon transform from steely gray, through the first rosy promise of the sun on the low-hanging clouds, until piercing solar rays crawl up and over the Cascades to illuminate our dew-laden, blue-and-yellow tent. The warmth on my cheeks stirs me into action.

Percolating a pot of coffee takes priority over heating water for instant oatmeal. Usually I am lackadaisical in the morning, but today I am anxious to evacuate this quasi-wilderness and reenter the backcountry. A few scantily clothed folks wandering down the trail from Sunrise further impel our departure, and I fervently crave the space where an ill-equipped sightseer cannot sprint back to the parking lot at the least hint of inclement weather.

Retracing our steps of the previous evening, we pause to allow a father and son to pass by on their trek out from Sunrise Lodge. The bright-eyed four-year-old is bubbling with excitement for his adventure in the wilderness, and he blurts out "Hello" to us, though his father hastens to usher him past us. Refreshing naïveté contrasts with suspicious tentativeness. Why can't we always retain such pure-hearted candor? I bid the youngster a "Good day, and enjoy your hike," in as jovial and sincere a manner that I can muster, then drift on, with a smile on my face.

Tortoiseshell butterflies flit about a swath of cascade asters, which adorn the path we had sped along last night. A half mile before Sunrise the trail redirects to the south, plummeting briskly into the White River canyon; the well-visualized, frothing waterway can be faintly heard churning far below, after it has poured out of the snout of Emmons Glacier.

At four miles long and one mile wide, Emmons Glacier is the largest of its kind on the mountain and, for that matter, in the contiguous forty-eight states. In consort with Rainier's other glaciers, it dwindled after the mini ice age, only to enlarge once more starting in 1953. Ten years later the expansion was accelerated by a colossal rock fall, originating from Little Tahoma Peak, that enshrouded the glacier terminus. (As the landslide was superficial and not involving the deep-seated, chemically altered rock, the flow didn't liquefy into a lahar.) Boulders caromed several miles down the canyon, nearly to the White River Campground. Under the cover of its new stony insulation the river of ice relatively sped down the valley, extending 1,591 feet farther by 1982. In the subsequent decade the forward impetus abated, and the glacier edged forward only ninety feet more.

Clearly this pulsating entity, called Mount Rainier, has a sinister side to its personality, for on a serene day in 1981 gigantic hunks of ice ricocheted down the mountain at over 130 miles per hour, into a company of twenty-nine climbers, killing eleven. When a small plane crashed on the summit in 1990 it became the tomb for the two tourists on board. (The plane eventually melted through thirty feet of ice and then submerged in the lake that is located 150 feet deep atop the peak.) In 1995, four climbers stumbled into one of Emmons's crevasses and died.

I would later discover that the recent death Josh spoke about (at Mystic Lake) also occurred on Emmons. Don and Joel had successfully attained the apex of Rainier via the arduous Liberty Ridge route, but as they were descending on the glacier toward Camp Schurman they both fell into a crevasse at the 13,500-foot level. A neighboring climbing group witnessed the accident, and found Don unconscious and Joel banged up but able to walk. Part of the team continued on to Camp Schurman, at the 9,500-foot level, to summon help. Heeding the call, Army Chinook helicopters from Fort Lewis airlifted nine rangers to near the summit level in the gathering cloud cover of the last light of the day, with four rescuers reaching the injured men by eight o'clock in the evening. They determined that Joel was able to hike safely down the mountain under his own power. Don was already deceased; the rangers bivouacked overnight and reclaimed his body the next day. Rainier can bestow extraordinary joy, or inflict tremendous pain.

After surveying the placid-appearing glacier and envisioning its many booby traps, we weave down the open ridge before forsaking the sweeping vistas for dense forest cover. Trickles, emerging from damp folds in the mountain, gradually coalesce into clear streams flowing through brushy ravines. The trail crosses over multiple small wooden bridges, but no water refill is required, as our coast through the cool mountain air does not induce sweat.

The rising momentum is readily palpable as we round the mountain's northeast corner and are propelled southward, witnessing a fresh face of Rainier being unveiled. In its thirsty eastern shadow the scattered trees and stones are devoid of moss. Unfortunately, the footpaths are crammed with hikers due to the easy accessibility via the well-paved road. The steady din of motorized traffic drones above the river's murmur; chrome and vibrant metallic blurs intermittently whiz by.

Three miles later, and 2,100 feet farther downhill, the trail pours onto the asphalt of the White River Campground. It had been tempting to camp here last night, specifically to sip, splash, and douse in the free-running tap water—no filtering required. However, stomping through the darkness would have been a major drawback and, more critically, we didn't hanker to plop our tent amid the "car campers" and their blaring stereos, screaming kids, satellite dishes, barking dogs, and humming generators. Our misgivings of it as a Wonderland Trail campsite aside, we do lust for the ready-to-use water and consequently dash for the restroom. How heavenly to brush my teeth and scrub my body, with the luxury of an endless supply of liquid and a porcelain sink at my disposal. After fifteen minutes of scouring and primping, I pick out the relatively cleanest clothes in my pack—which isn't saying much—and saunter back outdoors, at which point Patrick eagerly rushes into the bathroom to cleanse himself while I watch the gear. A car full of senior citizens seems puzzled at our rough appearance. Even in our current laundered state I am sure we are quite "ripe." Yet I doubt these elderly bystanders can apprehend the indulgence of washing here, instead of stooping over to rinse your hair with water poured from the cooking pot.

Notwithstanding civilization's perks, we are not keen to reassimilate into the masses of humanity. In fact, such thoughts foment dysphoria and irritability. While trudging along the asphalt of the White River Campground Road our conversation is either cantankerous or nonexistent. My boots feel heavy and clunky on the hard, black surface. Milky braided White River flows east along with us, and, pivoting my head to the right, I gaze longingly across the waterway at the flourishing forest of Goat Island Mountain. The serenity beneath the living canopy beckons me; I wish the path could have at least been placed in the woods atop the small embankment to my left. Hemlock, cedar, vine maple, and alder all prosper here, but somehow they seem manipulated by the industrial hand of man. It is disconcerting to continually peer over my shoulders so that this trip won't end tragically with my being struck by some reckless driver.

After a mile of listless plodding we finally arrive at the even busier Sunrise Road. The rustic, rough-cut stone bridge, which ferries automobiles over the turbulent river, is likely the only reason that we have been routed this way, and the 1927 vintage structure comfortably fords the wide, churning watercourse—a far cry from the tenuous beam fording South Mowich River. Fortunately, it is only a hundred yards more until we retreat from the mechanical world, where I feel vulnerable, back into the affable forest.

Though the trail parallels the highway for the ensuing mile I am relaxed in the benevolent embrace of fir and cedar. The cars whiz by totally oblivious to our presence. "I am a wild creature of the forest," I muse with a smile. Along the roadway, colt's foot hold their white flower heads proudly, like a fist at the top of an outstretched, strong green arm. In contrast, the shadow of western hemlock cools the tiny puff of white atop a slender stem balancing on the broad green frond of vanilla leaf.

We conclude our flight from the pavement at the Frying Pan Creek Access Trail junction. My spirit needs preparation so that it will be receptive to the therapeutic energy of the vital wilderness ahead. Hence, between bites of turkey jerky and gulps of kiwi-strawberry flavored water, Patrick and I try to dispel any negative emotions that have been generated by our brush with the fast-paced modern world. From the descriptions we have read, the upcoming stretch of trail travels through a wild, primeval forest that abounds with elk, bear, and goats. We are both excited to get back into the heart of Rainier, and the large biting flies chase us along.

Summerland awaits us 1,700 feet higher and four miles farther up the trail. The initial mile and a half are a nearly imperceptible rise through massive old-growth Douglas fir and silver fir, with prickly devil's club guarding their trunks. Those few small breaches in the canopy that do exist are overwhelmed by a dense, wet mat of grasses and thimbleberry briars.

Near the leap over a cool clear stream, we spot two pairs of discarded shoes and socks, and, with the proximity of the major road, we are vaguely apprehensive about psychotic weirdoes stalking unwary hikers in this secretive backwoods. But low and behold, just around the bend are the two retired fellows from Sunrise Camp, cooling their bared feet in the refreshing brook. A simple "hello" and nod of the head suffice, as we march on by, caught up in our irrational appraisal of this duo; both of us wondering if they are sizing us up in preparation for an ambush. My conscious brain discerns how silly that assessment is, but a more deep-seated instinct advises to not take a break for a while.

In short order we arrive at a ridge of durable rock, which has more effectively resisted the forces of erosion. The pitch steepens to overtake this obstacle, where Frying Pan Creek is slowing filing the flinty resistance into a narrow chasm; the dramatic vertical walls channel the racing water through a series of chutes that spray down into deep pools. Ferns cling to the damp, sun-deprived walls. A welcome by-product of the churning flow is a steady, cooling breeze that dissipates the few drops of sweat on my face.

After switchbacking through fir then groves of alder, we are treated to fleeting views of Mount Rainier straight ahead. Down the slope and across the stream to our left, the dark vertical precipices of the Cowlitz Chimneys guard against any direct southern assault. Where would I scale that formidable wall if there were no other option? I pause and search for topographic clues, trying to reconcile the lofty snowfields with the Sarvet Glacier fragments delineated on the map. Muted waterfalls cascade through the shadows. Surely there are goats grazing in the lush meadows that intervene between the ice, but alas, no.

Suddenly the forest relinquishes the ground to a tangle of huckleberry bushes, and, with the breeze in our faces and the brush obscuring immediate visibility, I am apprehensive that we might waltz right into a bear. It is a relief to gain the ridgetop, where we are granted unobstructed views of the streambed. In the shelter of this canyon, large patches of snow linger deep enough to have either completely engulfed, or hidden evidence of, the demise of the footbridge that reportedly crosses over the creek. In fact, where the span should be is now an imitation arch, fashioned by the stream boring a tunnel through the whiteness, and certainly not safe to risk shuffling across. Fortunately, a de facto trail has already been blazed through the dense willow shrubs and mountain ash, leading us to a safe ford.

We track the alien red ribbons upstream, past rosy spirea and Lewis monkey-flower, to a spot where we can conveniently skip over immovable rocks and a sturdy log to safely set foot upon the south bank. Bushwhacking up the bank we quickly regain the legitimate pathway, where a genial pair of middle-aged men greets us. Their faces are flushed and their breathing is labored from their recent exertions, but they have a secret to tell.

"Is the bear still here?" the lead fellow asks excitedly, but with a constrained voice. With receding hairline and rounded face he was probably more athletic in a prior decade, but now pursues fish from the cushioned seat of a boat; his companion is pudgier, and is sweating profusely in the direct sunlight. I have the impression that they used this strenuous hike as a ploy to escape from their families, forsaken back at the RV.

Their question prompts me to be instantly alert, scanning the thick brush for hints of a bruin's presence. "No. Why, did you see one nearby?"

"When we hiked up this morning there was a bear in the brush right near here. Just twenty feet from us. It didn't seem scared of us at all, and just kept right on feeding," he recalls with bravado. He intends to create the impression that the encounter was not terrifying, machismo, but even now he is mildly tremulous and shifts his eyes to give the willows the once over; undoubtedly the confrontation will be rich fodder for future campfire tales.

"Really? Was he big?" Patrick interjects.

"No, looked like a two-year-old. He clearly wasn't intimidated by us," he repeats. "We ran into another guy who saw the same bear when he packed in, so it must hang out around here," he concludes matter-of-factly, accompanied by a nod of his head.

"Those kind of bears make me nervous," I admit, to his apparent relief as with my disclosure his swaggering stance of squared shoulders and upright chin droops in confession, and fear emerges.

"I know," he almost giggles. "We heard noise coming up through the brush and thought we might run right into the bear, but fortunately it was just you guys." The image of an unexpected, intimate encounter with a bear has us all chuckling anxiously. Perhaps we shouldn't linger so long in the beast's lair. "Well, we better let you guys go," the lead chap proffers as they edge away.

"Yeah, thanks for the warning about the bear. I hope we get to see him—at a distance. Have a good hike out."

"You guys too." With that, they are chugging down the slope.

Left to ourselves in the suddenly perilous wildlands, Patrick and I expectantly survey the wide brushy meadow for telltale signs of the bruin. He is probably napping in the midday heat; I try to convince myself. I mumble half to Patrick and half to myself, "Those are the kind of bears I worry about. They get so used to humans that they stop considering you as an enemy, and we start thinking of them as Yogi Bear." Patrick acknowledges his agreement with a dip of his head, while simultaneously interpreting my facial expressions. I know his contemplation—if Dan is anxious, I should be anxious too.

To emphasize the point, I retell my bear story set in the Enchanted Valley of Olympic National Park. A few years ago I had packed into the breathtaking valley of a thousand waterfalls. The picturesque site was not only a Shangri-La for motivated human beings, but also was the steadfast haunt of a hefty black bear, which had lost all fear of people. The behemoth would amble through the meadow parallel to the trail I was treading upon, only twenty feet away. I am convinced he knew who the master really was; if he so desired, he could have been atop me in two seconds. (I still have a descent picture of him that I took while sitting in the doorway of my tent—not exactly the kind of material from which pleasant dreams are concocted.) The second morning that I was there I visited with a couple who had bedded down in the ranger's cabin. They too had seen the bear, and in fact the animal had approached to within an easy stone's throw of the porch. As he appeared friendly enough, the young woman tiptoed, with camera in hand, to within ten feet of the grass-eating creature. All went well until the brilliant camera flash startled the bear from his preoccupation, and he instinctually responded to the unforeseen threat by leaping forward, with ears thrown back and lips curled intimidatingly, toward the photographer. After a guttural *woof*, the bear did finally turn and trot away, but not before leaving the woman pale with fright. If you yearn for Yogi Bear, go to the circus; there are none in the wild. Nonetheless, I still hope to observe one here at Rainier, at least at a respectable distance.

Warily we step over fallen spruce trees and across hardened snow, until we start the final, arduous climb into Summerland. The last mile zigzags up a particularly steep hillside, upon which stout fir trees are interspersed with meadows containing patches of groundsel, subalpine lupine, and an occasional columbine. I monitor the progress of Patrick, who is gliding back and forth on the trail above my head, and finally catch up to him at a point where the trail rounds off onto the ridgetop and bursts into a profusion of color. The numerous white fluffy heads of post-prime pasque flowers and bistort, magenta paintbrush, pink mountain heather, and lupine accentuate lush green sedges sporting coffee-colored seed heads.

Summerland is a thousand-foot-high peninsula jutting from Meany Crest, to preside over Fryingpan Creek. To the west, the ramparts rise across Fryingpan Glacier, reaching the summit of Mount Rainier itself. To the north, above the Fryingpan Creek drainage, the rounded elongated hulk of Goat Island Mountain floats in the sky, devoid of humanity. To the east, the valley we just ascended falls away in an emerald forest carpet all the way to the White River and beyond. To the south is Panhandle Gap, the kingdom of rock, the various guises of water, and a few tenacious tufts of grass. Summerland is a boundary between mineral and carbon.

After hurriedly choosing a campsite and setting up the tent, we study the surroundings, and to our glee a small number of mountain goats are noted grazing serenely on the rugged slopes to the southwest. Grabbing the camera, we rush through the grass and lupine and ascend the trail in pursuit.

The Wonderland Trail climbs through Summerland

From here the path is a royal staircase to the paradise of rock, formed from a series of horizontal timbers; water oozes in, around, and over all. Five adult goats and two kids flit effortlessly among the tiny streams issuing from the dark gray cliff above us. The youngsters are especially boisterous, bounding amid the lemon-moss enshrouded stones, unperturbed by our presence. Kings of the bluff, their docility allows for an excellent photo opportunity. Finally we bag some big game! The white masters of the land of ice canter facilely across snow bridges as they climb toward Panhandle Gap, but our lungs battle the oxygen-deprived air, and it is difficult to keep up with the ungulates.

Our route requires a fifty-yard traverse over a snowfield, under which a ten-foot-wide creek can be heard cascading beneath our boots. Shortly we arrive at the shores of several tarns that reside in the glacial cirque at the head of the valley. Large chunks of bluish ice bob in one of the small lakes, at the base of a dwarf glacier, with delicate mosses and grasses clinging to the water's boundary. Ten feet away, the multihued gravel takes over the ground, though there are glorious displays of deep violaceous Davidson's penstemons cowering from the wind. High up the towering snow mass, the goats continue with determination, their heads slightly bowed down with the effort. Patrick and I regard them contentedly, and vow to return here tomorrow morning and hang out for a while.

The day's last sunbeams sparkle on the ice above and the evening breeze ruffles the tall grass far below, while we consider returning to camp. The older chaps from Sunrise tramp by on the final slog up to and then through Panhandle Gap. We wave in greeting when we glimpse them, then head down the hill in the opposite direction. Midway in the descent we are met by a young park ranger, who is looking for the two older men we'd been crossing paths with over the last two days. After we report, with some trepidation and curiosity, our most recent sighting of the pair, the ranger resumes climbing at a brisk clip.

"Did you see the gun he had?" Patrick talks in a hushed tone, while looking up the slope to be sure the ranger hadn't turned around; he is referring to the revolver prominently displayed in the ranger's holster.

"Yeah, I didn't realize they could carry guns," I reply over my shoulder.

Patrick, who is following me down the trail, declares with a sense of wonder, "You never know who you will meet out here."

"True."

"I told you there was something up with those two guys. They made me nervous," he continues triumphantly. Now that the ranger is well out of earshot, he is shouting from behind me loud enough that I will clearly understand him.

We are both reenergized by this late afternoon escapade and the good chi of Summerland, so I have a puckish smirk on my face as I jest with him. "So you think they are murderers or something?"

In response to which Patrick is mildly defensive, but compelled to further expand on his theory. "Well think about it. Maybe they robbed a bank or something. They could come out here and disappear into the wilderness. I mean, who would look for them here?"

"Yeah, Johnny and Guido. Fugitives from justice. What do you think will happen when the ranger catches up with them?" Well, I might as well play along.

"I don't know," he muses, "but if we hear gunfire, and the ranger walks by all covered with blood, I'm not saying anything." I glance back at his smiling face and we burst out in laughter. Quite the ridiculous scenario, but all in good fun; we are both dancing around in high spirits.

From our campsite we periodically monitor the trail for evidence that a crime has been committed. Of course we really don't believe our own tale, but still we are curious. I obtain water while Patrick finishes unpacking our gear. Following dinner we settle down with cups of almond chocolate flavored hot cocoa, just in time to see the ranger descending toward Summerland. He stops by to chat and make sure everything is going well here, and is clearly irritated that we are the only persons ensconced in the individual camping spots. While moving his eyes from site to site he bluntly questions us. "So have you guys seen any other packers here?"

"Well, it looks like someone is at the group site, but we haven't seen anyone else," I answer dutifully. At the same time I am more interested in what happened over Panhandle Gap during the last hour, though the ranger is obviously displeased with my report about the vacancies here.

"Summerland is supposed to be full tonight," he curtly retorts, but he is not upset with us. "We had to turn down two other parties who wanted to camp here, because all the sites are supposed to be taken," he seethes between clenched teeth. "If you guys come out through White River would you stop at the ranger station and let us know if anyone else showed up?"

"Actually, we're going the other way."

"Oh, okay. Maybe I'll check with the folks at the group site." His eyes no longer rove the plateau, but focus directly on us. "This is why people need to change their permit if they're not going to be where they signed up for. Others miss out." I am gratified that we had taken the time to have Jeri officially adjust our agenda, although I wonder how many of those that had scheduled to be here this evening had originally intended to complete the entire Wonderland Trail; somewhere along the way they deserted their dreams, perhaps pulling out cold and wet after slogging up to Mowich Lake, or with sore toes at Longmire, or sunburned and homesick by their arrival at Sunrise. In such misery, informing the rangers about the deviation in their course would be the least of considerations. Still others may have sped up their itinerary like us, taking a chance that other campsites would be open; they are now long past.

Unable to resist, I query the ranger. "So did you find those guys?"

He is caught a bit off guard, but quickly replies, "Yes. They have an off-trail camping permit and were setting up camp down in the valley on the other side of the pass."

"Cool." The rest will be left to our imagination.

"Well, I better get going or I'll be caught in the dark." After a firm handshake, his long strides carry him away toward the White River.

Watching him depart, Patrick and I discuss how superbly conditioned the ranger must be to power up from the road and dash back out every day; tonight he has less than an hour of dim light remaining to guide his way back to his vehicle. Most impressive! I assume he either runs or utilizes a flashlight; either way, I wouldn't want to barrel right into the bear along Fryingpan Creek, although he likely has a pet name for it.

With the last heroic day-tripper expelled, Nature lays bare her true wilderness personality. Patrick and I drift around our butte in the sky, snooping down on the meadows along Fryingpan Creek with the telephoto camera lens, scrutinizing for sizable mammals, but to no avail. The gregarious couple from the group camp joins us, doubling our survey efforts with their powerful bird-watching binoculars. The accompanying small talk establishes that Bob and Gretchen are from Vermont, and travel to the West every year for a two-week vacation.

"We come in the early fall," Bob explains. "Usually it's less crowded with everyone back at school."

"Yeah," I agree, "the backcountry can seem relatively deserted this time of year."

"It used to be better way back when, you know. The airplane rates were good, and there was no problem using frequent flier miles," Bob continues.

"That makes sense."

"But now everyone has figured out that this is a good time to travel. Even the airlines are raising rates and restricting the number of seats for frequent fliers." He seems forlorn about the loss of such a good thing. The secret is out: the hidden lake that only you knew about is now crowded by humanity. Most typical is the airlines cashing in on the popularity.

"Figures," I snort derisively.

"But we'll always find a way to get out here," he assures genuinely. "We've been camped here for a week, but this is to be our last night. Tomorrow we're going to find a nice hot shower and a Laundromat, somewhere."

He mentions soap and shampoo with reverence and a lilting voice, but his wife's face positively blossoms into a wide grin. "Finally, clean hair," she jokes. We all laugh with divine visions of hot water splashing on our heads, the delectable first scrubbing after a week in the woods.

"I know what you mean. Hot running water is going to be the first priority when we get out," Patrick adds enthusiastically.

Our attention drifts across the U-shaped valley to admire the golden complexion of forest and prairie in the day's good-bye kiss. I feel so calm, harmonious; the internal storms have blown away and serenity saturates the vacuum in their wake. The life force of Rainier permeates my essence. All existence is as it should be. Judgments are superfluous.

Bob breaks the silence by casually pointing over to Goat Island Mountain. "So did you guys see the elk herd over there?"

"No, are they usually there?"

"Last night we counted twenty elk in those high meadows," he gestures, demonstrating how they grazed uphill and then over the top of the mountain. "Let me see if I can spot any now." Bob lifts the binoculars, which had been dangling from his neck, up to his eyes and intently examines the dusky hillside. Elatedly he draws our attention to a small herd of wapiti, and we all take turns admiring the chestnut ghosts that silently glide across the highland.

"So how long are you guys out for?" Bob softly inquires.

"We planned on fourteen days to do the Wonderland Trail, but we decided to speed it up to thirteen days," Patrick recites the familiar refrain.

"So are you staying here after tonight?"

"No, we're going to Indian Bar tomorrow." Bob seems to be just curious, not expecting any specific answer from Patrick; no hint of puzzlement as to why we would proceed in such a manner.

"So you did a food drop at Sunrise?"

"No," Patrick answers sheepishly. "We didn't do any drops at all, though we definitely wished we did."

"Are you serious. No caches?" His mouth drops open slightly and his expression becomes more animated. At the time we plotted out this trip I didn't consider looping the mountain without a resupply station such a big deal, but it is clearly incredulous to Bob.

Patrick snickers in confirmation, "Yeah, no kidding."

"Wow! We have a friend back in Vermont, who came out here and did the Wonderland in six days, and he had only one food drop, and we were all impressed with that!" he explains sincerely. "Wait 'til I tell him about you guys doing the trail without a drop. He won't believe it." Shaking his head negatively. "I haven't ever heard of anyone ever doing it without a drop," Bob persists to the point of my embarrassment; I am not sure whether I should feel proud or stupid.

"Well, we definitely don't recommend anyone doing it this way. We wish we had a drop. In fact we've dumped food along the way to lighten the load," Patrick confesses.

Bob kindly adds, "Well, either way, it's impressive."

It suddenly dawns on me that Bob is one of those unique persons who always assumes the best, and therefore elevates every soul they contact; such jewels are rare indeed. Foraging through the totality of a life's encounters, the interaction with an individual whose every thought and comment is positive is rare indeed.

I am reminded of an episode a few years back, when a friend and I were riding the ferry through the Inside Passage of Alaska from Haines to Prince Rupert, and, to save money, we declined a berth and instead slept on the deck. Our tent was absurdly gargantuan, taped to the deck for all to see, and we had to sit in it most of the time to keep it from being blown away by the gales, so I couldn't deny my association with it. Every person who came on board stared, pointed, and otherwise guffawed at the hideous dome of nylon, while I shrank back in embarrassment. The German tourists set up their deck chairs next to the tent to use it as a windscreen. Yet there was one man who made a point of complimenting us on our fine tent. "It must be quite roomy and comfortable inside. The perfect sun and wind block. We should all be so lucky." He was quite serious and not phony in the least bit. I strive to develop such adroitness and compassion. Are these saints, who believe only the best of people, born that way or can that marvelous talent be learned?

By now the last faint rays of sunlight have abandoned the white dome of Rainier, leaving us to the darkness. We ingenuously bid Bob and Gretchen a pleasant night and hope they have a fun-packed remainder of their trip, and they wish us luck on our journey, before we all head back to our respective campsites by the beam of our flashlights and retire for the night.

The next morning we arise to an intense bath of golden sunlight. Camp is quickly taken down while the coffee is brewing. When the last cup of java is drained, we clean up the site and enthusiastically commence the climb to that splendid tarn-studded basin preceding Panhandle Gap. Now that we are not being hurried by a sunset we can leisurely explore the area. Along the windswept ridgelines toward Summerland, twisted subalpine firs furnish shelter for sedges from the harsh weather. In the more immediate surroundings, brave flowers punctuate the coarse pumice. Large bright flowers of golden fleabane resemble a broad smile; the familiar rich red leaves of Newberry's knotweed brighten the gravel; low growing mats of penstemon are enshrouded with tubular flowers in hues of rose and lavender; and patches of alpine lupine, pussy-paws, and stonecrop are randomly strewn hither.

Two ponds adorn the cirque. The closest, which is hunkered at the base of a vertical glacier, is icy blue and deep, with the chunks of ice, observed last twilight, still floating around within it. The second pool is situated slightly downhill from the first, away from the snowfield so it is devoid of ice, with a rim of diminutive jade grasses struggling to survive beside its shallow waters, a most foreign land.

On the far side of the second pond an impressive male mountain goat reclines on a mossy cushion. At such close quarters his size exceeds my expectations, and, though wary, he conveys no fear of our proximity but only exudes confidence in himself. He lies on his right side, with his left front leg casually stretched out in front of him—composed and at peace. The ebony spiked horns are threat enough; dark eyes placidly appraise his habitat.

The ungulate's photograph secured, I go about further exploring the terrain while Patrick locates a sturdy rock on which to meditate. Eventually I too plop down with my back against a boulder and analyze my sentiments for this stark landscape.

Why do we feel such a strong connection with rock and dirt and ice? To me there is a visceral bond, but not with just any stone. The essence pervading at Panhandle Gap has unexpectedly evoked in Patrick a soul-soothing oneness. He meditates, contemplates, and otherwise communicates with this entity, as if he had run into a long lost friend. Why do I love thee? It's not the sweetness of your water, or the light reflected off your crystalline walls, or the wind blowing through your snowy crest, or the heat rising from your rocky bosom. No, beauty penetrates much deeper. I love the whole of your being in all its immensity.

This mountain was begot from some small crack in the earth from which molten lava surged, much the same as I began from a small seed that expanded into my being. All of existence is an organized accumulation. Pulverized, I am just a pile of hydrogen, oxygen, carbon, iron, calcium, and potassium. I am water, tree, and rock. I am mountain, forest, and sea. I am not static, but continually exchange myself with the whole of the world: eat, drink, breath, sweat, defecate, urinate. Earth flows in and out with a regular rhythm.

The atoms I have captured have migrated about the universe. My last drink contained hydrogen that melted from five-thousand-year-old ice that formed from evaporation of the Pacific Ocean, which flowed down a river in India that originated from melting glaciers in the Himalayas, ad infinitum. The carbon in the apple I just ate was processed by a tree that sprouted in soil swept down from a Cascade mountain, which flowed up with magma from the mantle that was conceived by the Juan de Fuca plate melting under the North American plate. Atoms do not live *and* die; they transform, pair up, mix and match, evolve, and devolve in a complicated dance. I am a collection of voyagers, which have been the inside of a star and drifted through the vastness of space to coalesce into me; soon enough they will continue their voyage through the cosmos.

Perhaps it is my human arrogance that presumes I am seizing the atoms for my discrete wont. Like the huckleberry employs the bear, perchance the atoms utilize me so they may move about the universe. It doesn't have to be purely chance that a particular carbon is in a berry that I happen to eat, or a peculiar oxygen exists in the water I sip. With the knowledge of eternity, conceivably they positioned themselves enticingly right where they knew I will pluck them, and, once on board, they experience what it is like to be human. Sooner or later they will shove off to another perspective. I feel rewarded that so many have chosen me, and I aim to be an excellent host.

I hope my molecules speak well of their captivity, and I like to think that they have a memory. Perchance they may tell stories of their existence; if I abide humbly, they may murmur their tales to me. Theoretical physicists suggest that there may be eight or more dimensions, of which we know only four: forward-backward, right-left, up-down, yesterday-tomorrow. Perhaps atoms reserve the other four for their own amusement. They now whisper to me. "You *were* once that rock. You *were* once that drop of water. You *were* once that blade of grass. Our memories are yours."

No wonder I weep for a chain-sawed tree, a polluted stream, a dynamited mountain. To rip a butte asunder for a few pounds of gold tears away at my soul. "Can't you do something?" my mineral contingent screams. Yet here, in the serenity of this scene, they murmur lovingly, "Yes, Yes."

Indian Bar

The first paradox...There can be no effect without a cause. Whatever events transpired near the outset of time, each must have been caused by some prior event. So we can never attain an account of the very beginning.

TIMOTHY FERRIS, *THE WHOLE SHEBANG*

The sun has drifted well beyond midday, and we dutifully, yet reluctantly, leave this soul-stirring domain. All sensations are heightened; the patches of magenta paintbrush seem much more vivid; the dry air burns my lungs pleasantly; the dusty incense of pumice wafts round my nose dreamily; the mountain breathes in gusts of wind that rise and fall.

The trail ascends from the tarns, with the finale edging along the cusp of a sheer snowfield before cresting at Panhandle Gap. Sweeping grandly to the southeast the treeless bowl of Ohanapecosh Park funnels downward through meadows and krummholz to coalesce in the Ohanapecosh River. The name means "looking down on something wonderful," and though it supposedly originated with a Native American warrior peering at his reflection in a pool of water, the view from here incites that expression. Somewhere beyond the waterfalls and ridges lies Indian Bar.

We linger at Panhandle Gap in a final embrace with this wondrous arena. A middle-aged man strides by; he hardly has time to say hello, otherwise he risks failing in his ambitious day-hiking plan. Soon after, we monitor the progress of another lightly clad hiker trekking by the lakes and then across the snowfield to overtake us where we now lounge. He is a talkative, thirty-something fellow from Seattle with a free weekday, courtesy of his charitable boss. The chap has elected to spend his gift on an impromptu expedition to Summerland, following his whims. He retells stories about prior adventures in Nepal, Chile, and Antarctica, which stir up reveries of future excursions for Patrick and me, but soon enough he strikes off cross-country in quest of the mountain goats grazing along the Cowlitz Chimneys that we had pointed out to him. Such serendipitous interactions make for an enriching life, full of wonder and exploration.

Patrick at Panhandle Gap

164

Patrick has the restless mien of a nomad, and I know we must be moving on, but my feet shuffle in meager protest and then halt to oblige a liberal inspiration. A mass of sooty clouds, borne on an approaching cold front, has narrowed the braid where sky meets land, which is further blurred by a bluish haze billowing up from the myriad of canyons. In the depths of these gorges flows Rainier's contribution of life-giving fluid, heading south to mingle with the milk from Mount Adams's glaciers. The massive dome of Tacoma's cousin sails above the obscurity to our south.

At my feet, the white-and-red-tinged pompoms of pussy-paw hesitate to lift up into the cool winds. Tiny alpine lupines ply the expanse of pulverized lava, dispersed among fields of buckwheat, whose leaves are ablaze in autumn crimson. To the east of Panhandle Gap, a wide grassy plateau slopes up to clash with the rugged Cowlitz Chimneys, before veering southeast to Double Peak and then diving abruptly to Chinook Creek. Employing my telephoto lens, I can spy the wayfarer from Seattle stalking the lofty meadows in pursuit of the goat herd; the nimble cliff-runners are placidly moseying along in the direction of Double Peak, before I lose sight of them when they round the hillside. My eyes rove down through the basin, doggedly probing the prime forage for bear and elk…but the denizens are elsewhere. Oh, well.

I release a lengthy sigh that vibrates to my fingertips and triggers my legs to propel my body southwest, across the loose gravel and semipermanent snowfields. Occasionally the trickle of a submerged brooklet can be heard underfoot, but we traverse all snow bridges safely. Despite the absence of paint-splashed rocks or cairns, the proper route is confirmed by the line of dirty, melting footprints. Patrick and I perform a leapfrog of consensual autonomy, sharing thoughts and discoveries at our intersections.

A two-hundred-yard, icy, uphill stomp wraps up our climbing requirements for the day. Beyond a small escarpment to the west of our apex, the formidable Ohanapecosh Glaciers hold their chunk of the mountain in place. However, the water they discharge is restless, plunging off a vertical, gray cliff into an abyss from which courses the Ohanapecosh River. Curving southeast, we hump down the spine of the ridge that divides the ravine on our right from the sweeping watershed on our left. From this vantage point I can distinguish an alien lithic square, Indian Bar Shelter, plopped within a large meadow a mile down the canyon; that is our goal for the day.

The trail bisects small clusters of spruce and subalpine fir, shielded by the lower elevation; however, the majority of the ground is blanketed knee-deep by an incredible wildflower display. Bare ground is nonexistent, and even our path is masked by the uninterrupted pageant of brilliant red paintbrush, indigo broadleaf lupine, puffy white seed heads of pasque flowers, bistort, pussy-paws, pearly everlasting, mountain arnica, and pinkish mountain daisies.

Mountain goats at Indian Bar

Just above the altitude of camp we catch sight of numerous mountain goats across the waterway to our right, where they are feeding serenely on the lavish grasses growing at the base of a five-hundred-foot-high wall of dark, gray rock. The escape route afforded them by the cliff undoubtedly enhances their comfort level. I count thirty-seven fine white animals in this group, including several rambunctious kids deftly bucking and dashing about the heath and talus. With this bounty of sensory stimulation the distance to the streamside meadows rolls by effortlessly.

The guidebook portrays black bears romping round this stage of blossoms and young, stray silver firs in the glow of twilight, while we partake of the show from our seats at the cottage. And quite a theater this is, with many gurgling tributaries draining into the roaring torrent. On the fertile banks lining the gravel bed reside thick patches of Lewis monkey-flower, mountain monkey-flower, aster, lupine, corn lilies, and groundsel; lemon-lime mosses cloak any residual gaps. Water ouzels bob nervously as they hop from stone to stone within the stream, then dive into the swift current in pursuit of insects, only to emerge five feet away from where they submerged. All the water rushes into a narrow defile of the smooth rock, which breeches the ridge damming the meadow. We cross over the channel on a sturdy bridge and troop thirty yards up to the hut.

Indian Bar Shelter is a solid-appearing structure built by the CCC in the 1930s. The miscellaneous rocks have had their rough edges chiseled to fit and then assembled like a giant jigsaw puzzle; rough-hewn timbers square the doorway and bolster the cedar shingle roof. A wobbly picnic table is positioned just to the right of the entrance. Behind the shack, a timber and dirt stairway leads abruptly up to an outhouse that has no walls, back, or roof; there is only a porcelain seat to squat upon and admire the unobstructed view of the entire terrain we ranged over this afternoon.

This is hardly a ghost town, as folks are bustling all about. On the bluff beyond the miniature chasm (that we cut across to get here) are several brightly colored nylon tents, whose tenants have descended the slope across the river and now are in the "bear" meadow. The four young women are walking side by side, meticulously searching the ground for—we will ascertain later—bugs. They are participants in a university research program that has permission from the Park Service to scour these meadows in an effort to catalog the diversity of insects. Soon they are joined by a professorial-appearing gentleman, who promptly guides them up the gravel streambed, sloshing through the river with the protection of their waterproof boots to, presumably, snare gadflies.

Dan relaxes at the Indian Bar Shelter

Turning our attention toward the shelter, we greet four college-age guys who are awaiting our arrival. Of the quartet, only one fellow actually converses with us, but then again he rattles on enough for all of them. Regarding the aloof three, one is stretched out supine with his head on a rolled-up jacket and a baseball cap shielding his face; the second is wandering around the immediate vicinity with the pretense of stretching his legs, while he monitors the progress of the young ladies wading upstream; the third comrade is sitting cross-legged by the sealed-off fireplace within the dwelling, diligently stirring a liter pot of boiling ramen noodles. When the pasta is fully cooked, he spoons equal portions into four plastic bowls and then distributes the meals to each pal, along with the requested flavoring packet. This basic sustenance is consumed ravenously by all except the talkative one.

The incessant communicator is ensconced in the doorway, and after tossing our packs into the rear of the building, we plop down to join him. He is slightly overweight, with mild acne and wire-rimmed glasses adorning his face. Per his discourse, we learn that they initially intended to spend most of their time here, or at Summerland, but the sites were already filled. So instead, they looped east from White River Campground to camp at forested Deer Creek Camp and then followed the Eastside Trail to Olallie Creek Camp. He assures us that this alternative route, in part because of the marvelous swimming hole at the latter site, has not disappointed them.

Today they had a tardy departure but, despite it being five o'clock already, are still aiming to wind up at Summerland, five miles distant. Surprisingly, he doesn't seem too miffed when I tell him that the campground was practically vacant last night and they could have had their pick of sites.

Within a few moments they have polished off the ramen, expeditiously collected their gear, and reembarked on their trek. Over the next half hour I catch glimpses of them trudging single file through forest, meadow, and the high ridgeline from hence we came.

It is a relief to finally have the campsite to ourselves, though the solitude is transient. Ascending from the bridge is a slender, fortyish man in blue jeans and navy blue polo shirt. At his heels, dressed in shorts and a T-shirt, is a teenage youth of Native American lineage, who pauses beside his mentor to chat with us before they head up to their camp, which is located somewhere beyond the toilet. The goal of their foray is to methodically prospect the valley for Native American artifacts. (Bands of the Cowlitz tribe still hunted here as recently as 1906.) Perhaps the teen is interested in discovering some vestige of his heritage, and I wish them good luck in their undertaking, as chronicling historical cultures is a noble endeavor. Although, if nary a soul exists to give flesh to that civilization, the documentary seems only to be a conqueror's entertainment.

As our neighbors roam away in their diverse pursuits, Patrick and I attend to the tasks of setting up camp. The first order of business is to suspend all our perishable supplies from the rafters of the shelter, using the nylon rope we had bought. Patrick is somewhat skeptical, but I have yet to run across a backcountry shelter devoid of resident mice, and the rodents tend to be voracious and ingenious; crawling up the walls and nibbling through canvass to claim their treat. The flat, packed-dirt floor is inviting, so we elect to forgo the tent in favor of spreading our sleeping bags out in the open air.

Over the western ridge, thick clouds are gliding in and the wind has a chilly nip, making the hot chocolate and hot spiced cider all the more gratifying. By the time we finish eating dinner and dessert, twilight has abandoned us to darkness. Under cover of the starless night the Native American youth cruises past in the direction of the biology students' tents; good-natured giggling from across the creek soon flutters through the darkness to our ears. Inside the shelter a plump pack mouse is foraging about for any crumbs we may have cast aside. I flash the light in his beady eyes. "What did I tell you," I proclaim triumphantly to Patrick. A slithering sensation creeps up my legs, and we both agree that it would be a good idea to put up the tent within the shelter, because neither one of us wants to wake up in the middle of the night with mice crawling over our bodies.

I feel like a pioneer, secure in this solid stone structure. Out there bear, elk, deer, goats, cougar, fish, birds, insects, and all the minute organisms of the world rove the beneficent slopes of Rainier in quest of individual survival—and ultimately, the future well-being of their species. Each and every one of them is a link between the past and the future. I reflect upon the biologists scrounging about in the meadow and streambed on a mission to understand the lives of the smallest creatures, and the archeologists groping for the remnants of a society not yet buried. On the timeline of creation to infinity, the present is such a thin sliver.

The second paradox: You can't get something from—or for—nothing. The "origin" of the universe, if that concept is to have any meaning, must create the universe out of nothing. Therefore there can be no logical explanation of genesis (Timothy Ferris).

The clouds are swirling around the volcano, the trees are swaying in the breeze, and the river continues to churn, unaffected by the sun's absence. All existence is in motion, a constant haphazard evolution...even Mount Rainier.

Once again, I imagine the ascension of lava from a level swampy plain. The explosive adolescence thrusting it high into the atmosphere. The calm of maturity allowing plants, animals, insects, fish, and reptiles to prosper. The thick sheet of ice age glaciers slowing melting away to reveal the beautiful dome. The ebb and flow of the remnant rivers of ice scooping out the valleys. The landslides tearing away the peak's flesh, only to have eruptions rebuild it. Finally the influx of Native Americans, and then, in the last wink of an eye, the arrival of European-Americans.

The naming of the peak, its glaciers, its rivers, and its sub-peaks for those who alighted only in the most recent twitch of the mountain's life is shallow. The assignment of those nineteenth-century labels strikes one as being the work of the conceited—chest-thumping subjugators. The Native Americans' style of honoring the mountain with eponyms that denote its importance, including to the sustenance of those people who abide on its flanks, seems much more appropriate. I have no idea who Admiral Rainier was as a man, whereas I can easily visualize the mountain in the role of the "mother of the milk-white waters." When Van Trump was informed that the Park Service wished to apply his surname to one of Rainier's glaciers, his response was not to pridefully boast, but instead to utter, "I am opposed to applying the names of men, even great ones, to mountains, rivers, glaciers, or any of the sublime things in nature." Human epithets are merely whispers, like the ticking of a clock, not representative of the longevity of the mountain.

Homo sapiens are a rather trivial species in the grand scheme of planet Earth; we are not the dramatic climax of the universe's life. Listening to the tumbling river it occurs to me that we are rather like a drop of water circulating through an inconceivably complex world, but that doesn't mean I can't wonder.

The unsolvable riddle that is our universe has often spawned anguish in my problem-solving brain. If it is dilating, then it must possess a boundary, but what constitutes that verge? Furthermore, into what is it expanding; what exists beyond the perimeter? The supposition that something could subsist without an end is incomprehensible, but if matter is contained, then some substance extends outside of the container; that is the absurdity of infinity. Theoretical physicists must all surely lose their sanity!

The babble of the perpetually flowing stream echoes from out of the midnight gloom, reminding me of the magical and eternal cycling of live-sustaining water. Perhaps our souls are like a drop of the liquid, swirling from eddy to eddy of bodily animation, with the sundry conditions and pressures changing one's composition. Life is but a momentary borrowing of the elements, much too small to fathom, much too broad in time to comprehend.

If I am a drop of water, then is the universe I call home a tumultuous entity like Mount Rainier? A growing lad, experimental adolescent, or young adult struggling to attain nirvana, it absorbs, incorporates, and enlivens that which it impacts, with the unused mass being pulverized, vaporized, and discarded. The exponentially inflating cosmos mimics a bomb detonating in the ocean, generating a halo of powerful swirling currents that soothe the ambitious mass. Once maturity is obtained, what then, oh universe? Will you succumb to your inner frailties, be crushed by the turmoil you have created in the sea of your existence, or simply, silently wait for Nature to reclaim your body? Atom by atom, quark by quark. Height is magically lost; mass flows out.

Decay begets fertile ground, which nourishes new life. The elements, including time, are immortal. Life eternally cycles, even on the cosmic level. John Gribbin discusses in his book *In the Beginning* that our universe may be a living entity with an extended family. Similar to a flower propagating seeds, a universe procreates via its black holes. Each singularity grows into a different, unobservable dimension, but greatly resembles its parent universe, for the fact that it carries its parent's genes in the form of its unique physical laws. Akin to the individual pearly everlasting plants we observed along Kautz Creek, which emphasize the characteristics it requires to prosper and reproduce in its specific locale, each baby universe would do the same. So you see, the universe can be finite and infinite together.

The third paradox: Regardless of its net energy, the universe must have originated from another system, and that system must in turn have had an origin of some sort. And so we are caught in infinite regress (Timothy Ferris).

To stare at its broad snowy dome, Mount Rainier also gives the impression of strength and immortality. Nonetheless, its interior and exterior are eroding away, and it is primed for explosive change. The volcano's turbulent personality has crafted awe-inspiring features to which humans have affixed their tacky names. In spite of the fact that the titles will likely survive longer than the persons will, eventually the mountain will remodel itself and eliminate the denoted landmarks: melt Emmons Glacier, erupt and bury Hessong Rock. I should venerate this creator, and all the breathing and no breathing entities that thrive on its shoulders. I endeavor to be at peace with the universe, and not inflict it with painful wounds during my sliver of time here. The future happiness of the atoms in my body may depend upon my sanctity.

The Wonderland Trail has captivated me with its flowers, trees, birds, soil, rock, water, and ice. With the impact of each footfall I have been brought into contact with incredible scenes that have imprinted indelible pictures within my mind; but more than good memories and sore muscles, this loop has brought my soul back into the spiritual fold of our living universe. I perceive, somewhere inside of me, the biting arctic wind blowing through the subalpine fir, the beaming smile of a golden fleabane basking in summer's brief light, the joy of a mountain goat kid nibbling spring's sweet grass, and the turmoil of this mountain entering the throes of midlife.

The trail has also led me through the ghosts of the past. Magma surging up to rebuild the devastated mountaintop, and lingering as steam vents that rescue intrepid climbers who cower on its summit. The pre-Rainier swamp solidifying into coal and sandstone deposits that were subsequently mined by early European pioneers. The intermingled societies of Yakima Park. Soo-to-lick striding the cultural bridge to become Indian Henry. The witty nomenclature of Ben Longmire. Outburst floods rasping sores in the Kautz and South Tahoma Creek Valleys, which scab over only to be scratched open again. I have sensed the phantasm of William Tolmie within Spray Park, Edsel drivers having lunch at Carbon River Camp, and the tales of white-goateed Van Trump echoing from the rotting debris of the Wigwam Hotel. Glorious Sunset Park is not at the pinnacle of an evolution, but is the agglomeration of all that it was, and all that it will ever be. The past and present are indivisible. The concept of time is meaningless here.

I strain to visualize the Mount Rainier of tomorrow. What future explosions and landslides does it plan? Will it burgeon, or slowly wear away to an inconsequential hillock? The answers surround me now in the essence of the trees, ice and rocks; they know their destinies. The knowledge of eternity is present already in my atoms, though my brain will never comprehend.

Patrick and I chat contentedly from our warm sleeping bags, within the pitch-blackness of the nylon dome, enveloped by the sheltering stone hut, tucked under the wing of one of Rainier's harboring valleys. I feel safe, bundled in this haven of the eons. It is a solid, dignified, fulfilling aura, and I am so very fortunate to share the world with such a special entity.

Circling the base of Rainier has been much more than a physical workout or get-away-from-it-all trek; it has reminded me that I am a tiny part of an immense, loving universe. Life ebbs and flows between all beings, and I can find comfort in the arms of the cosmos.

Complacency does not usurp realization, as my atoms are restless; got to move on to the next experience, the subsequent existence. Patrick and I agree to arise early tomorrow morning and start walking, and see if we can complete the final twenty-one miles back to the car. My body aches from the exertion of the trip, but my mind slumbers tranquilly.

Race To Paradise

The heavens themselves run continually round, the sun riseth and sets, the moon increaseth, stars and planets keep their constant motions, the air is still tossed by the winds, the waters ebb and flow...to teach us that we should ever be in motion.

ROBERT BURTON, *THE ANATOMY OF MELANCHOLY*

Overnight the clouds have thickened and descended with their load of moisture to drape the Cascade Mountains; instantly transforming them into the gray and dreary pattern of autumn. A cool, steady drizzle threatens to metamorphose into snow. We are fortunate to be protected in this dry shelter while packing our gear. After the final cup of coffee is drunk, I stash the pot and cups into the top of my half-filled backpack, then reluctantly don rain pants and Gore-Tex jacket, before cinching the rain cover on my pack. All bundled up, we begin the ascent out of Indian Bar.

My mood is somber during the initially steep, then more gradual, one-mile climb to an exposed, rocky saddle. I am reticent to mention out loud that we are rounding the final corner of Rainier, and soon will be sprinting along the southern leg toward Longmire. Wasn't it just yesterday that we clambered up Rampart Ridge?

The showers have abated, so we pause to peel off the suffocating raingear. The chilly, damp air feels good against my legs. For the next three miles the trail contours along the crest of a ridgeline, rising and falling over eight mini-summits. There are brief strolls through subalpine fir thickets, but the majority of the time is spent ranging through open meadows. To the south, Mount Adams's summit is secreted in the low-hanging, drab, cumulus clouds; cloudbursts fashion sporadic curtains that soften the distant landscape in between. As we proceed southeast, the Cowlitz Chimneys, across the valley to our left, thrust their rocky crags into the atmosphere in silent salute of our departure, though the mountain goats have forgone the adieus. Behind us, grassy pastures at the base of Rainier tempt us to hazard an off-trail shortcut to Paradise, but we resist.

Halfway along the ridge, we fortuitously peer down from a five-hundred-foot-high cliff to spot two elk stomping through a streambed, in flight from some invisible threat—probably us. Quickly they melt into the far hemlock forest. It is hard to believe that overzealous hunters exterminated the native Olympic elk from the slopes of Rainier. The animals below are the descendants of a few Rocky Mountain elk brought here in railroad cars from Yellowstone (1912) and Jackson Hole (1933). Closer by, fresh deer tracks are frequently detected in the heavy pumice of our pathway, and their splayed hooves indicate they fled posthaste. It seems that we are disturbing the casual breakfasts of a multitude of animals.

The appearance of humble Bald Rock on our left heralds the terminus of our ridge run and the exodus from the high country, as we descend back into the verdant forest. To indulge one last gasp of the rarified air we opt to take a break at a small overlook, ten yards off the trail. (Undoubtedly, this is the first open vista for those hikers ascending from Nickel Creek.) We drop our packs and gander down into the abrupt meadow, and are startled by a black mass looming out of the corn lilies and golden sedges. The first and only black bear we have encountered during this sojourn is a hundred feet below, munching contentedly on the grasses, totally unaware of our presence. We hurriedly fumble for our cameras to snap a few photos, and then settle down to just watch.

Serendipitously, at precisely this moment, the first person that we have met today comes hiking briskly up the trail and hesitates when he detects our presence. A truly auspicious rendezvous, for if we had not crossed paths at this juncture he would have sped by, woefully unaware of the bear's proximity. Quieting him with a finger to my lips, I wave him over, and the trio of us spy on the beast for a few minutes before it becomes suspicious. Suddenly the bruin raises his head and sniffs the air purposefully. Within seconds he has pinpointed our position, and then pivots to scamper away in the opposite direction, to be swallowed up by the dense, protective forest. I wonder if the spirit of the mountain has rewarded our diligence and goodwill with the special sights of this morning.

From here the route swiftly drops through a variety of ecosystems. Subalpine fir and spruce yield to red cedar and mountain hemlock, before we switchback down into the massive old growth of Douglas fir and western hemlock; vine maples once again line the small brooks and moss clings to the trees. The completion of our journey is palpable in the reversion to the type of woodland resembling that at our jumping-off point.

It is late in the morning when we tramp into the campsite at Nickel Creek, although we have no intention of setting up the tent now, but merely desire to desist from our march long enough to doctor sore, blistered feet and nibble on residual, stale jerky. The rotten remains of an aged, wooden shelter rests on the level plateau, twenty feet above the cold clear waters of twenty-foot-wide Nickel Creek. The air is clammy and oppressive with the evaporation of the morning's raindrops, captured by the overhanging trees and tangled undergrowth that contrive a temperate jungle. It is the perfect environment to refresh our hot, sweaty, and now bare feet.

In this misty realm the bones of fallen giants are languidly decaying, dust to dust; the unselfishness of the arbor vita manifests itself. Having successfully competed for prime canopy sunshine, she sprinkles offspring seeds around her body, and then collapses so that they might thrive upon her flesh. In her last throes she devises a clearing so that sunlight can flood to her children and ensure their prosperity. Perhaps the universe is a mother tree—expanding to create space, nourishing her seeds of black holes, which sprout off into their own time and dimension.

Neither I nor physicists should quarrel so vehemently as to whether the universe will ultimately collapse, balance precariously, or expand eternally, for the truth may be none of the above. It is conceivable that seedling universes (black holes?) are feasting on the flesh of their mother, who is past her prime. If I were a microbe firmly ensconced within the trunk of one of the fallen giants currently around me, then that which is outside of the tree's bark would be a profound mystery not to be fathomed. The appearance of fresh tendrils, manifesting the tender roots of a new generation, would be quite puzzling, as the youngsters are sprouting beyond my field of vision. They surge forth into another time and dimension, scavenging planets, stars, and galaxies, via the firm clutch of black hole gravity, to fuel the growth. Praise for the children! Don't fret for the proud mother.

The sense of completion catapults me forward. Shortly after crossing the bridge spanning Nickel Creek the trail intersects with asphalt again; however, the grandeur of the Box Creek Canyon defile is only minimally lessened by the extensive parking lot and paved walkway leading to its viewpoint. As we meander along, I inspect the lime-yellow moss and stone-crop clinging to a flat slab of rock; cedar trees predominate in the immediate woodland. From the platform of a sturdy wooden bridge stretching across the chasm, I can see the turbid waters of the Muddy Fork of the Cowlitz River thundering downstream, 180 feet below me. The vertical walls of the grotto are only fifteen feet apart, but they are adorned with a multitude of ferns and sedum. It is an amazing sight that speaks volumes to the power of erosion. Across the canyon we climb over a hillock—through which the road tunnels—that is a natural overpass for those traveling on foot.

Awaiting us on the other side is a relatively level stroll through a wet forest of vine maple, red alder, and hemlock. Here, at the base of the mountain, the streams are swollen by the aggregation of all the lesser tributaries cascading down from the ice and snow aloft. Stevens Creek swirls through smooth, glacier-carved bedrock beneath an umbrella of cedar and western hemlock. Stabilizing the banks are stately red alders that lean to and fro of their own whim. Without prevailing winds to shape them (which we saw with the krummholz), they are left to the manipulations of the liquid currents tugging on their roots, and the competition for sunlight pulling on their crowns. Their trunks are splashes of white, black, and many shades of gray, with green mosses clutching in the shadows. A secondary track bolts through the shady timberland toward a nearby picnic ground, which reminds us that from here to Longmire we will be in the company of the well-traveled highway. It is an admonition that, though this is beautiful terrain, it isn't pure wilderness.

The ensuing mile glides through the placid woodland, with the winding Cowlitz River off to our right. That substantial waterway twists and turns through its braided, rocky channel, yanking alder trees into the flow to form calm pools in the swirling water. One of the few horizontal segments of the Wonderland Trail ends in the vicinity of Maple Creek Camp.

The camp is situated on the nearside bank of its namesake stream, and consists of four clearings, nestled in a grove of young hemlocks. By the evidence of the well-trampled earth, the fourth spot must be the most popular. It is the farthest upstream, and is positioned on elevated turf at the edge of the forest, affording an excellent view of precipitous Stevens Peak and overlooking a dense tangle of salmonberry bushes. I'm sure a few hikers have had an apprehensive sleep, wondering if a bear was stalking them through the brush.

Maple Creek is our last legitimate opportunity to set up camp for the night. We have descended three thousand feet over ten miles to get here, but it is still another eleven miles to our car, including a 2,000-foot ascent, before the final 2,200-foot plunge to Longmire. My back and legs are sore, as are Patrick's, but the die is cast; my mind has already determined that it will be exiting the trail today.

So after a brief respite, we struggle back under the packs and commence up the moderate slope. Accompanying my escalating heartbeat is the distinctive *meeep, meeep, meeep* of a dump trunk going in reverse on the highway, partway up the sheer mountainside across the valley to our right. The mechanical beast comes into view simultaneously with the metallic *thunk* of its tailgate releasing, and the subsequent resounding dusty tumble of a load of crushed rock bounding down the hillside. The sound of busy automobile traffic is altered by a Doppler effect as the vehicles whoosh in and out of side canyons. Nature's murmurings seem lost in the shuffle of mankind.

When the peaks close in we are forced to traverse rough talus slopes and battle through a horde of berry bushes. The sun emerges from the clouds long enough to bake the vegetation, which consequently releases a heavy dose of chlorophyll that permeates my nostrils. A mile later we waver at a side trail off to our right, which leads to Sylvia Falls, but we decide not to investigate. Subsequently, the pathway steepens significantly, skirting along a flinty cliff, then reentering a dark brooding forest, before arriving at the spectacle christened Martha Falls by Ben Longmire, in honor of his mother. (Actually, there are two cataracts in series on the voluminous stream, each falling approximately forty feet.) Patrick volunteers to scale down the crumbly bank, below the burly planks of the bridge, in order to replenish our water supply. Our conversation has dwindled to a bare minimum as we concentrate on our individual exertions.

I do not want my joints to congeal, so I drop off my pack, but continue to shuffle about for the duration of our fleeting reprieve. Once the challenging ascent resumes I lag behind Patrick, and he eventually disappears ahead of me; we each need to establish a tolerable pace within our respective comfort zones, especially as our muscles fatigue. I am using landmarks to gauge my progress and distract my brain from the labors of my body. The guidebook describes Unicorn Creek Bridge as being a half mile beyond Martha Falls, but when I have gone at least three-quarters of a mile up the abrupt incline, I realize that Unicorn Creek is only a good-natured joke, inducing a jolly chuckle from me. After the first crossing of the Stevens Canyon Highway, ripe thimbleberries yield to robust and extraordinarily sweet huckleberries, goading me to perform the huckleberry two-step. The guidebook promises that it is less than a mile from here to the top.

Lake Louise

Patrick is stoically waiting for me where the trail again meets the road, and together we amble on the level grade parallel to the highway, circumnavigating the western shore of Lake Louise. Autumn has erupted in a kaleidoscope of reds, browns, and yellows—subalpine firs provide contrast—that paint the talus slides soaring skyward from the far side of the pool. The calm water creates a mirror image of the showy exhibition in the hazy late afternoon light.

Arcing around the basin I recognize the modest pass that marks the culmination of this trip's final climb, tantalizingly close; unfortunately, ground-hugging pallid smoke is shooting up over that ridge, harbingering stormy weather. Upon attaining the crest we are immediately engulfed in dank, frosty fog. The steady, biting draft abruptly convects heat out of our bodies, with the aid of our perspiration-soaked clothing. The fleece and Gore-Tex apparel are a feeble stopgap, considering that I start to shiver whenever I come to a standstill. We plod along the shores of Reflection Lake, with drenched views of rosy spirea, pearly everlasting, and marsh marigolds; but Mount Rainier is invisible in the murk. In fact, the far bank of the tarn is not even consistently discernible. Our route hugs the road and its litany of cars, out of whom a series of souls protrude to snap off a few photos; in the dim light, most travelers simply stop and stare briefly out of their windshield before moving on.

Upon arriving at the western outlet of the lake we toss aside our packs and refocus our thoughts. My eyes flick across the pages of the guidebook in an attempt to peruse the final chapter, but hypothermia and fatigue numb my attention. From our prior studies I vaguely recognize the highlights: Narada Falls, Paradise River Camp, Carter Falls, and the Nisqually River. Instinctually I crave warmth, and hence strip down to bare skin. The trade of cold, sweat-drenched clothes, for the driest shorts and long-sleeve shirts present in my pack, ministers a welcome feeling of wellness. I am fortunate to be well provisioned with gear that stands up to the elements, so I feel physically tested but not endangered. But how does one know when they have gone beyond mere discomfort and entered dangerous ground?

Reflection Lake

In my limited experience it seems that it is the mind that gives up before the body is defeated. Here I am in a delirious, visceral misery after having tramped over sixteen miles in mildly inclement conditions, yet I am cognizant that my body has not touched its reserve, and if I cease the hike now it will be because of my self-preserving consciousness. Most people never push their body to its ultimate potential, perhaps only doing so at death. Kautz, Van Trump, and Stevens must all have wondered whether they had crossed that mortal divide as they struggled in their wet, cold, weathered threads toward the apex of mighty Rainier; but instead of being sad footnotes in history, they were elevated to legendary status. I do not want notoriety but, on the contrary, pine for the luxuries awaiting me at the Jeep.

I set the pace as we sail downhill with urgency; only two hours of light remains to complete the final five-plus miles to Longmire. The heavy clouds will effectuate an earlier dusk, and I don't want to be hiking by flashlight. The landmarks blur by; Narada Falls can be heard booming through the massive western hemlocks. Three wooden bridges (104 feet, then two of 43 feet each) ford the Paradise River, but no thought is even entertained of stopping to join the group camping there. I do feel somewhat guilty in speeding through this area that the local natives called Saghalie Illahe (Land of Peace).

The Paradise River Valley is indeed a wonderful environment, but our footing is chancy on the slick rocks and tree roots as we barrel down the steep hillside. Alder trees and salmonberry bushes fringe the smaller waterways; along the slopes grow massive mountain hemlock, yellow cedar, and silver fir, with a dense understory of devil's club, rhododendrons, Oregon grape, and huckleberry bushes; tucked in between are ferns and bunchberry.

Halfway to Longmire, we scoot past Carter Falls and begin to encounter a multitude of day hikers, who are casually strolling about enjoying the scenery. Most have walked a mile or two, at most, from Cougar Rock Campground and various roadside trailheads. Eagle Peak rises above the talus slopes across the river to our left. The vine maples growing in the clearing are flaunting brilliant reds and yellows, confirming that we have trekked two weeks from summer to fall. On the day we had embarked on our journey, I remember wondering what it would be like wandering through this canyon, and now I know. The satisfaction of completion is experienced with a warm rush.

Raspberry bushes and vanilla leaf make an appearance when the trail levels off and pivots around Ricksecker Point to the juncture of the Paradise River and the wide channel of the Nisqually River; this murky river falls rapidly from its namesake glacier up near Paradise. The gravel bed is denuded of vegetation, and I am positive that it is a raging torrent during spring's melt-off. A succession of lengthy, log platforms covey us safely over the multiple braids of the river.

Across the last scaffold we take a final, brief recess in a tiny parking lot alongside the highway. From here it is a rolling descent along the river to Longmire, and when the forest reverts to the variety of old growth indigenous to the trailhead region I know we are close. Houses peep through the trees just before we overtake the trail junction that we had passed twelve days ago; however, we do not linger to reminisce in the dreary twilight. But as I plod the concluding strides to the Jeep, I apprehend deep in my heart that this has been much more than a hike around some mountain. It has been an honor to share a fraction of existence with Rainier, and marvel at all that treads upon its bountiful slopes.

Patrick arrives at the Jeep

We quickly dump the packs into the vehicle, wash up in the public restroom, and change into snug cotton attire. With a ravenous hunger, we burst into the National Park Inn only to have the hostess regretfully inform us that the dining room is closed and that there are no beds available for the night. As a consolation she telephones Paradise Lodge and is surprised to discover that they have one room vacant and the dining room will be open for another hour, though she doubts we can get there in that time. She has discounted the powerfully motivating sensation called starvation. We muster the strength to run to the car and speed up through the oppressive haze.

Dan at the end of the trail

184

Paradise Inn

The most essential elements of medicine power are: ...A belief in a total partnership with the world of spirits.... The possession of a non-linear time sense. A receptivity to the evidence that the essence of the Great Spirit may be found in everything. A reverence and a passion for the Earth Mother, the awareness of one's place in the web of life, and one's responsibility toward all plant and animal life. A total commitment to one's beliefs that pervades every aspect of one's life and enables one truly to walk in balance.

BRAD STEIGER, *INDIAN MEDICINE POWER*

By the time we get to the top, the fog is so thick that we can't even tell where the inn is from the parking lot. Emerging from the vehicle we are lost in the surreal scene, and blindly follow those people who are striding with confidence and purpose, like tracking an army of ants. Suddenly the lodge entrance materializes out of the murkiness. A soft yellow light effuses from the large window panes, behind which folks are reading, chatting, playing cards, and strolling about admiring the architecture.

The door is a portal into a reminiscent taste of a bygone era. Eighty years ago adventurous souls celebrated the opening of this grand inn, which was built to eliminate the inconveniences of the preexisting tent city. It is constructed in the Park Service motif of rustic, but elegant style.

Stepping through the threshold we advance into the great hall, where thick boughless trees support the steepled roof, three stories overhead. On the second floor is a ten-foot-wide catwalk rim, where people are also lounging around the small wooden tables. We turn to our left and pass the couches and chairs huddled near the crackling fire that is roaring in the sturdy, stone fireplace; however, there is not enough time to examine everything now, as hunger implores us to hurry.

Between the fireplace on my left and the check-in desk on my right is the doorway into the equally grand dining room. Patrick confirms with the host that we still have some time to clean up and return to eat—fifteen minute to be exact. It seems fortuitous that we got the last room in the entire park; it was just meant to be.

Hefting our duffel bags, we rush to our right beyond the front desk, then past the stairwell to the second floor, before entering the passageway to the guest quarters. The staircase we descend and the whitewashed hallway we trot through are all askew—resembling the slanting floors and tilting walls of a circus funhouse. A faint vertigo besets me, but perhaps that is because my brain is adjusting its visual-spatial sense after having been in the unconfined outdoors for the last two weeks.

The room is actually two chambers connected via an antiquated bathroom. Upon opening the entry door we are met with a blast of chilly air; therefore, while Patrick showers, I turn on the heaters before shaving. The clock is ticking and my appetite must be sated, ergo this scrubbing is only cursory—just enough to be presentable to the paying public. The blue jeans and cotton shirt feel foreign to my skin.

Adequately cleansed and dressed, we dash back up the drafty staircase, past the front desk, then through the glass-paned doors and down a few steps into the dining hall. It too has a vaulted ceiling supported by rough-hewn logs, akin to the great hall. Cold, frothy microbrew amber ale tastes delicious; bruschetta, prime rib, and a fine Merlot soon follow, so that my tongue is dancing with its revival from the customary pasta and hot chocolate.

With a toast to our success I first comprehend that the adventure is over, the course has been run. After all the planning, training, and organizing, we have actually pulled it off. The Wonderland Trail wasn't exactly what I expected; no, it was so much better than anything I could have imagined. All the details have been etched in, the passing personalities expounded, the weather presented, and the myriad faces of Rainier unveiled. Eagle's Roost was heavily wooded, not some rocky perch; afternoon clouds routinely rolled up through the western valleys, while Summerland basked in unfiltered sunlight; people hiked by alone and in groups, fast and slow, for a day or two weeks, women and men, teenagers and senior citizens; twilight blushed on the jagged glaciers of the lofty mountain. Serendipity is the key to happiness, delight in each experience as it occurs; forget the agenda.

Fully satiated, we casually saunter back toward our bungalow with placid spirits, despite our legion of somatic pains. We are greeted by a blast of arctic air when our door is thrown open, and I momentarily wonder if the room was available because it is haunted. But alas, the culprit is an open window in the second chamber. My sleep is certainly tormented, but not by spirits. Tylenol and Aleve barely lessen the deep, writhing ache that throbs through my spine and hips—the advent of dawn is such a relief.

Crawling out of bed and into the shower, I let the hot water beat between my shoulder blades to massage my spasmodic muscles. Reluctant joints are maneuvered into shorts and a sweatshirt, and then we hobble up to the mess hall for a smorgasbord breakfast of American favorites, which render substrates my muscles require to initiate their healing. After the leisurely meal, and being in no hurry to depart, we climb to the second-floor balcony and play cards at a quaint writing desk overlooking the fireplace in the great hall. The inn supplies coffee and herbal teas on this level, free for the taking, to warm your hands and gullet.

Between sips of java I inspect the sizable, stripped cedar logs that constitute the framework of the 50-by-112-foot hall. The weathered timbers have a story to tell, a tale about order out of chaos. That which appears to be an absolute disaster may ultimately be just another beneficial event for Tahoma.

One day old Ben Longmire was trying to scorch a nest of yellow jackets near Ricksecker Point when wind caught the flames and whipped it into a major conflagration. An old-growth forest of yellow cedars was burned to a crisp, but time and the elements transformed the charred ancients into a rustic gray, similar to those we had observed near Golden Lakes. Yellow cedar wood is exceptionally resistant to degradation by insect and weather alike (which is why it is prized for construction), so when Paradise Inn was envisioned, the ready supply of sun-dried timber provided the ideal raw materials. The ghostly snags were transformed into this classic park lodge, and the living forest is recovering quite well in its own right. So what is the disaster? It was only a catastrophe for those who are shortsighted.

Inch-thick steel cables are situated about the lodge in a bid to stabilize the structure, attempting to prevent its collapse, pushing back the day when fungus, mold, and worms will reclaim the carbon of these old trees. It wasn't intended to be immortal, removed from the exchange of atoms. The eventual demise may be gradual or precipitous; after all the inn is built on the two-thousand-year-old debris of the Electron Flow, and another landslide could sweep the lodge to the sea. That notion reminds me that we all awash in a current of energy, not separate from it.

People of a variety of ethnicities and ages drift to and fro through the lobby below, like the ocean tide. As it is mid-September the children are gone, but college professors, retirees, young vagabonds in sweatpants and shirts, and couples elegantly dressed in the latest wool sweaters and fine trousers all mingle among the tables and couches and warm themselves aside the flames.

The thousand-acre meadow of Paradise has hosted the rendezvous of a diversity of humankind through the centuries. Nisqually berry encampments were superseded by the tents of the "Camp of the Clouds" and subsequently the fortification of this wondrous inn. In 1922, the slopes were abuzz with the first Motorcycle Hill Climbing Contest. The following year a laundry facility and ice cream plant were constructed. A boat rental concession and general store were organized at the Reflection Lakes in 1927, and by 1931 there were 275 cabins, a golf course, snowshoe rental facility, photography studio, horse stables and corral, in addition to the guide hut that had been erected in 1920. Plucky skiers, taking advantage of the rope tow to swoosh amid the powder overlooking the lodge, and dog-sled teams enlivened the invigorating winter atmosphere. Competition energized the renowned slopes in 1933 with the Silver Skis Race from Camp Muir to Paradise—a five-thousand-foot fall in less than eight minutes—and peaked with the Olympic Ski Trials and National Downhill/Slalom Championships in 1936. The Paradise Ice Caves, tunneling through the body of the Lower Paradise Glacier, were a popular attraction until the shrinking mass made the passages unsafe, necessitating the closure of the routes by 1971, and the glacier itself did not exist by 1993. (The uncovered earth was colonized by seven different plant species within six months.)

In a microcosm of the planet, Mount Rainier is resilient to the minor transgressions of humanity, provided that its core integrity is preserved. Mankind's amusements merely scratch the surface of the volcano, wounds that can be easily healed. Even roadways gouged into the flesh of the mountain are being reabsorbed, as we observed at North Puyallup River and Carbon River Camp. Rainier is not static.

Over the last twelve days Patrick and I have beheld many natural splendors and encountered a cross-section of the human race. All were unique and interesting, but we will never meet any of those folks ever again. What happened to them? What experiences did Rainier afford them? I wish I could hear their tales.

Will Tom ever plan an entire vacation around climbing a mountain again? Did the mother and her four kids finish the loop, or did they exit early and seek out a shower? How far and fast did Steve hike? Have any of the Northern Loop aficionados from Mystic Lake developed an ambition to complete the Wonderland Trail? When will Josh scale a Himalayan peak? What was the real history of the two older gents from Sunrise? Where will Bob and Gretchen go next year? Have the biologists found their bugs, and the archeologists their artifacts at Indian Bar?

People come and go with unknown pasts and uncertain futures, but all that I will ever know of them is the brief moment we shared on the slopes of Mount Rainier. That is not a melancholy thought, for we each have our own path to traverse, and if we focus on the present, instead of the past or future, it will be an enriching journey. I have learned, with every interaction, about deep-seated human instincts: the apprehension and intrigue of strangers, the fear of darkness and loneliness, the suspicion of other's intentions, and the joy of a pure human heart. Utmost is the realization that *Homo sapiens* are not the climax of the universe, and we have less control than we think we do; hence, we should relax and enjoy the ride. We should live within the bounds of the ecosystem and not battle it.

Every day, human beings scurry about here. (In fast motion, it must resemble ants on an anthill.) Once freed from the ice age glaciers, humanity has swarmed about plucking the fruits of Tacoma. Native American tribes, European explorers, American settlers, foreign tourists, and unimaginable future tenants and visitors will leave their rapidly eroding footsteps—countless heartaches and triumphs, pain and pleasure, struggles and rewards, hunger and satiation.

The Wonderland Trail has introduced me to the vitality of Mount Rainier. The dome stands stoically, but vulnerable; it is not a passive and terminal existence. Western society desires the world to be static and predictable, so that we may proclaim ourselves conquerors and the rulers of all domains. If Rainier were to explode today and wipe out all of Paradise, the nation would passionately mourn the loss; newspapers and television would positively weep. The area, however it settled, would become a memorial, complete with interpretive center—at least once it was safe to set foot here again. But the tears would not flow forever, because Nature's work is not a catastrophe, that thought is myopic, but it is a dynamic process of transition that benefits the planet Earth.

From the ashes of future eruptions will arise a new forest to wipe away the tears of lament. A pristine summit will be molded to gather the rain; fresh, resplendent meadowland will drape the slopes in a scintillating display of color and aroma; seedlings will spring skyward into old growth in but a blink of the mountain's eye. Another generation of bear, elk, deer, and all the other children of Mother Nature will walk, fly, and swim on the volcano. And yes, our children and grandchildren will come to explore. Perhaps they will come as conquerors intent on gracing features with their moniker, but I hope they recognize the volcano for what it is—a dynamic, volatile, yet beneficent and gracious entity. Let us not disgrace it by titling it after its parasites, but instead acknowledge its value to the Earth.

A thousand years from now Rainier will undoubtedly be altered, but less so than the minor beings crawling over its flanks and scaling its dome. Civilizations will have risen and fallen; glaciers will have grown and retracted, grinding stone into soil for transport to the sea. I pray that we will have exercised enough restraint to have saved, and perhaps even expanded, the diversity of breathing beings here. As photographs flash by and the album pages turn, I hope the images displayed will be more beautiful, wilder.

In that interval my atoms will have diffused throughout the universe, carrying their memories of this wondrous place and time. Re-assimilated in some future beast, raindrop, magma rise, or *Homo sapien*, they may feel compelled to return here to quench a mysterious thirst: How is Mount Rainier now?

The energy of the universe pervades all of us; accordingly our goal should be to facilitate the mutual prosperity of the planet's co-inhabitants, and stop being so arrogant and stupid as to think that we know what is best. Quiet observation reaps great rewards. We interact with the perpetual flow of atoms, and hence ascertain our place in the cosmos. Erecting dams across the atomic stream may indeed create lakes of stagnation in which all will flounder. I fear our souls will not have a healthy universe in which to grow. I fear that Nature's garden will become weedy and forsaken.

My body, my atoms, my soul have all matured in their association with this tremendous peak; I will never be the same. Mount Rainier, the volcano, will also evolve. Landslides, forest fires, glaciers ebbing, lava flowing, and eruptions may all greatly alter the dome within my lifetime. I can never return here seeking the same experience as that which occurred over the last two weeks. Happiness lies in the future. I must keep moving, though perhaps my atoms already know the secrets of tomorrow and the coming millennium. Eternity is here at Tahoma.

I deliberately survey the great hall, its gray timbers lashed together in a vain attempt to resist the pull of gravity. Through an open window, on the third-floor level, blows a cool mist– source of erosion, hypothermia, lifeblood to the firs and moss, substrate for snow and glaciers. I have no animosity toward the fog; instead I feel the harmony of the mountain's environment.

Down below in the lobby, people scurry about in search of some inner peace. Do they curse the haze in their lives, or accept it as a nourishing agent of growth? I wonder if Rainier has helped identify and clarify their membership in the cosmos like it has me—no better or worse than a drop of water, shrew, or stone. I hope they have felt the interconnectedness of all that surrounds them: history coursing through the woods, streams, rocks; human culture, geology, and biology; past, present, and future are intertwined. I feel my atoms and soul have experienced this perfection before, and hope my present essence will ensure joy for future beings. The soothing warmth of all that has been and all that will be permeates these flowers of the universe. I pray that my life will lead to the perfection of Nature's garden.

With a satisfying sense of completion Patrick and I pack up, check out, and drive down out of the fog. Rolling past the trailhead at Longmire evokes whimsical memories of our first steps onto the trail; Kautz Creek is crossed again, but this time by automobile; Ranger Brown's cabin is a blur as we accelerate out through the park gate. Patrick peers over at me and asks, "So where do you want to go next time?"

Reflection Lake and Mount Rainier on a sunny day

Bibliography

American Park Network. "Mount Rainier National Park: Flora and Fauna, History, Lodging and Dining, Geology, Lodging and Dining, Sights to See." Internet site: www.americanparknetwork.com/parkinfo/ra. Meredith Corporation, 1996.

Barnes, Christine. *Great Lodges of the West*. Bend, OR: W W West, 1997.

Berry, Thomas. *The Dream of the Earth*. San Francisco: Sierra Club Books, 1990.

Brown, Tom Jr. *The Tracker*. New York: The Berkley Publishing Group, 1979.

Carpenter, Cecelia Svinth. *Where the Waters Begin: The Traditional Nisqually Indian History of Mount Rainier*. Seattle: Northwest Interpretive Association, 1994.

Chasan, Daniel Jack, Tim Thompson, and Thomas E. Lovejoy. *The Smithsonian Guides to Natural America: The Pacific Northwest*. Washington, DC: Smithsonian Books, 1995.

Chatwin, Bruce. *The Songlines*. New York: Penguin Books, 1988.

Clark, Ella E. *Indian Legends of the Pacific Northwest*. Berkeley: University of California Press, 1953.

Daniel, John. "The Long Dance of the Trees." *Wilderness*, Spring 1988: 19–29, 33–34.

Davidson, Steef, postscript ed. *How Can One Sell the Air?* Summertown, TN: Book Publishing Company, 1980.

Driedger, C. L. "Glaciers on Mount Rainier." Open File Report 92-474. US Geologic Survey, Department of the Interior, 1993. wwwdwatcm. wr.usgs.gov.

Eckert, Allan. *The Frontiersmen*. New York: Bantam Books, by arrangement with Little, Brown, and Company, 1970.

Ferris, Timothy. *The Whole Shebang*. New York: Touchstone-Simon & Schuster, 1998.

Filley, Bette. *The Big Fact Book About Mount Rainier*. Issaquah, WA: Dunamis House, 1996.

————. *Discovering the Wonders of the Wonderland Trail Encircling Mount Rainier*. Issaquah, WA: Dunamis House, 1993.

Gribbin, John. *In the Beginning*. Boston: Little, Brown, and Company, 1993.

————. *Schrodinger's Kittens and the Search for Reality*. Boston: Little, Brown, and Company, 1995.

Hardin, Terri. *Legends & Lore of the American Indians*. New York: Barnes & Noble Books, 1993.

Krakaur, John. *Into the Wild*. New York: Anchor Book–Doubleday, 1997.

Krutch, Joseph Wood, ed. *Walden and Other Writings by Henry David Thoreau*. New York: Bantam Books, 1981.

Leopold, Aldo. *The River of the Mother of God and Other Essays*. Madison, WI: University of Wisconsin Press, 1991.

Little, Elbert L. *The Audubon Society Field Guide to North American Trees: Western Region*. New York: Alfred A. Knopf, 1980.

Livingston, John. As referenced in *Temple Wilderness*. *One Cosmic Instant*. Houghton Mifflin Company, 1973.

Lopez, Barry. *Arctic Dreams*. Bantam Books, by arrangement with Charles Scribner's Sons, 1989.

Lovelock, James. *The Ages of Gaia*. New York: W.W. Norton & Company, 1995.

Meany, Edmund, ed. *Mount Rainier: A Record of Exploration*. New York: The Macmillan Company, 1916.

Millman, Dan. *Way of the Peaceful Warrior*. Tiburon, CA: HJ Kramer, 1984.

"Mount Rainier, Washington: A Bloom in Paradise." *Backpacker*, February, 1990: 48–49.

Muir, John. *The Eight Wilderness-Discovery Books*. London: Diadem Books; Seattle: The Mountaineers, 1992.

Niehaus, Theodore F., and Charles L. Ripper. *Peterson Field Guides: Pacific States Wildflowers*. Boston: Houghton Mifflin Company, 1976.

Peterson, Roger Tory. *Peterson Field Guides: Western Birds*. Boston: Houghton Mifflin Company, 1990.

Rohde, Jerry and Gisela, and Larry Eifert. *Mount Rainier National Park: Tales, Trails, & Auto Tours.* McKinleyville, CA: Mountain Home Books, 1996.

Romanyuk, Tatiana V., Richard Blakely, and Walter D. Mooney. "Cascadia Subduction Zone: Two Contrasting Models of Lithospheric Structure." quake.wr.usgs.gov/study/Crustal Structure. Menlo Park, CA: US Geologic Survey, 1998.

Schullery, Paul, ed. *Island in the Sky: Pioneering Accounts of Mount Rainier 1833–1894.* Seattle: The Mountaineers, 1987.

Scott, Kevin, and James Vallance. "History of Landslides and Debris Flows at Mount Rainier." wwwdwatcm.wr.usgs.gov. Water Fact Sheet: USGS Open-file Report 93-111, 1993.

Seattle Times Staff and Associated Press. "Mount Rainier climber killed." *The Seattle Times*, 30 July 1997.

Simpson, Joe. *Touching the Void.* New York: HarperCollins, 1998.

Spellenberg, Richard. *The Audubon Society Field Guide to North American Wildflowers: Western Region.* 12th ed. New York: Alfred A. Knopf, 1992.

Steiger, Brad. *Indian Medicine Power.* Atglen, PA: Whitford Press, 1984.

Teale, Edwin. *The Wilderness World of John Muir.* Boston: Houghton Mifflin Company, 1975.

Petrie, Tom, Kim Leighton, and Greg Linder, eds. *Temple Wilderness.* Minocqua, WI: Willow Creek Press, 1996.

USGS/Cascades Volcano Observatory. "Description: Cascade Range Volcanoes." "Description: Composite Volcanoes and Stratovolcanoes." "Description: Juan de Fuca Volcanics." "Description: Mount Rainier Volcano, Washington." "Description: Mudflows, Debris Flows, and Lahars." "Description: Osceola Mudflow, Mount Rainier, Washington." "Description: Plate Tectonics and Sea-Floor Spreading." "Juan de Fuca Ridge—Gorda Ridge." vulcan.wr.usgs.gov. USGS/Cascades Volcano Observatory, Vancouver, Washington, 1997.

"Volcanoes: Mount Rainier." davem2.cotf.edu. Wheeling Jesuit University/ NASA Classroom of the Future, 1997, 1998.

Walder, Joseph, and Carolyn Driedger. "Glacier-generated debris flows at Mount Rainier." wwwdwatcm.wr.usgs.gov. Volcano Fact Sheet: USGS Open-File Report 93-124, 1993.

Watts, Tom. *Pacific Coast Tree Finder.* Berkeley, CA: Nature Study Guild, 1973.

Whitman, Walt. *Leaves of Grass.* New York: Bantam Books, 1983.

Whitney, Stephen R. *A Field Guide to the Cascades & Olympics.* Seattle: The Mountaineers, 1983.

Wolfe, Linnie Marsh ed. *John of the Mountains: The Unpublished Journals of John Muir.* Madison, WI: University of Wisconsin Press, 1979.

Made in the USA
Monee, IL
07 August 2022

11130535R00115